Illustrated Shakespeare

Romeo and Juliet

Editor: Neil King, Hymers College, Hull

Stanley Thornes (Publishers) Ltd

Other titles in the Illustrated Shakespeare series:

Macbeth
A Midsummer Night's Dream
Julius Caesar
The Merchant of Venice
Twelfth Night

Notes and questions © Neil King 1989
Line illustrations © Stanley Thornes (Publishers) Ltd 1989

First published in 1989 by:
Stanley Thornes (Publishers) Ltd
Ellenborough House
Wellington Street
CHELTENHAM GL50 1YW
England

99 00 01 02 03 / 10 9

British Library Cataloguing in Publication Data
Shakespeare, William, *1564–1616*
   Romeo and Juliet. (Illustrated Shakespeare series)
   I. Title   II. King, Neil   III. Series
   822.3'3

   ISBN 0–85950–843–9

Typeset by Tech-Set, Gateshead, Tyne & Wear
Printed and bound in Great Britain by
Redwood Books, Trowbridge, Wiltshire

Contents

Acknowledgements   iv

Foreword by Amanda Root   v

Preface to this Edition   vi

Romeo and Juliet

    The Prologue   **1**

    Act I   **2**

    Act II   **25**

    Act III   **46**

    Act IV   **71**

    Act V   **85**

Sixty Activities and Questions   100

Notes on Productions of *Romeo and Juliet*
  Illustrated in this Edition   103

Young Vic 1987–8

This edition is for Jonathan Forster.

Acknowledgements

The author wishes to acknowledge the help of many of his students, and especially Niloy Acharyya, Owen Houlston and Suneet Joseph, in the preparation of this edition.

The author and publishers are grateful to the following for permission to reproduce material:

Derek Balmer, pages 1, 31, 38, 42, 44 (left), 49, 51, 53, 57, 68 (right), 73, 94, 97, 98 • Birmingham Public Libraries, pages 2, 13 • Sheila Burnett, pages iii, 17, 20, 23, 50 (right), 74 • Laurence Burns, pages viii (bottom), 4, 9, 36, 37, 40, 50 (left), 55, 64 • the Syndics of Cambridge University Library, pages 12, 54 • Citizens Theatre, photograph by Edward Sykes, page 48 • Nobby Clark, pages viii (top and centre left and right), 63, 80 • Donald Cooper, pages iv, 70 • Chris Davies, page 87 • Robert Day, page 44 (right) • Fotomas Index, page 25 • Ivan Kyncl, pages 65, 82, 91 • Angus McBean, page 24 • Patrick Mackle, pages 14, 16, 35 • The Mansell Collection, pages 18 (bottom), 27, 28, 86 • Gerry Murray, pages 8, 11, 83, 90 • Geoffrey Newcombe, pages 58, 68 (left) • Orchard Theatre, Barnstaple, photograph by George Tucker, page 32 (left) • Oxford University Press for the woodcut by Roy Morgan reproduced from the *Poetical Works of Edmund Spenser* edited by E. de Selincourt and J. C. Smith, published by Oxford University Press 1961 © Oxford University Press 1961, page 10 • Paramount Pictures Corporation for *Romeo & Juliet*. Copyright 1968 by Paramount Pictures Corporation. All rights reserved, pages 34, 46, 56, 71, 76, 85 • Redgrave Theatre, pages 6, 21, 32 (right), 60 (left), 72, 88, 89 • Royal Theatre, Northampton, photographs by John Roan, page 30; and cover • Shakespeare Birthplace Trust, pages iv, viii (four), 50 (left), 63, 65, 70, 80, 82, 87, 91 • Shakespeare Centre Library, pages 15, 29, 39 (photograph by Bertram Park), 60 (right), 77, 81 (Tom Holte Theatre Photographic Collection), 93, 95 (photograph by Gordon Goode), 96, 102 • Solihull News, pages 41, 61, 66, 67, 78, 96 • Paul Thompson, pages 5, 18 (top), 27 (left), 28, 47, 62, 69, 99 • Desmond Tripp, pages 19, 45, 59 • Victoria and Albert (V & A) Museum, pages 7, 43, 52, 92 • Victoria Theatre, Stoke-on-Trent, page 22.

We should like to acknowledge the assistance given us by the Shakespeare Birthplace Trust and the theatres whose productions of *Romeo and Juliet* we have illustrated.

Every effort has been made to contact copyright holders, and we apologise if any have been overlooked.

. . . me, past hope, past cure, past help! (Act IV Scene 1 line 45)

Amanda Root as Juliet, Royal Shakespeare Company 1984

Foreword

Romeo and Juliet is probably my favourite Shakespeare play. Although not critically regarded as one of his finest works, the spirit of the piece rises above any minor faults the scholars may find.

The criminal waste of life so young, especially when it is only the death of the two lovers that reconciles their families, and the fact that the two lives sacrificed both possessed an insurmountable joy for life and love, can only make the story of *Romeo and Juliet* one of the greatest tragedies and heartbreaking love stories of all time.

In 1983 I was asked to play Juliet for the Royal Shakespeare Company. Fresh out of drama school, I was completely bowled over by my good fortune. I began rehearsals with excitement for the part and enthusiasm for the people I would be working with in this famous theatrical establishment.

As with any play, my initial response to it influenced how I approached the part. I had wept when reading *Romeo and Juliet* and I wanted our audience to have the same reaction to the play. I wanted them to be similarly angered and touched by the loss of innocence and life within that petty family feud.

Shakespeare's characters leap off the page. As an actress embarking on playing Juliet, I wanted her to live through my characterisation as much as she did from Shakespeare's text – I wanted to be totally convincing. It was also immensely important to me that when I came to speak Shakespeare's wonderful verse that I would deliver his lines in their full glory – not fumble through them because of any inability of my own.

Most actresses who play Juliet are inevitably considerably older than the 'real' Juliet. Although I was 21 when I played the part this was still comparatively very young to be taking on the role. I knew I would not seem 13 if I tried simply to 'play young'. My method for 'ageing down' is to bring out those qualities that have become modified and tempered as we get older. It's almost a freeing process – to delight in the hopes of youth again – that wild imagination and impulsiveness, the huge capacity for thought and joy and love! Shakespeare writes so brilliantly that he creates a very believable young girl – I just had to follow his directions and surrender myself to them. Once started it becomes quite easy to get in touch with those emotions. I never wanted to seem to be *trying* to be young, I simply wanted to *be* young.

I was aware that Juliet has a phenomenal journey to make during the course of the play – bourgeoning from a young girl into womanhood. The remarkable discoveries she makes of herself, her family and the world, and the rapidity of these discoveries, mean that she emerges in a very short period of time from a guileless child dictated by her parents into a young woman, independent and capable of deception. Although equipped with an innate maturity from the start she has further distances to travel in terms of her emotional development.

I loved the idea of a girl whose gift of expressive imagination, one of the very beauties of her nature, could turn and work against her. Juliet herself recognises the dangers of this ability when she tries to conjure up a never-ending night with Romeo (Act III Scene 5) and witnesses Romeo give himself up to her imagination.

He would be prepared to die if she wished it so. In this scene, faced with the hard reality of their hostile world, she has to give up the joy of fantasy into another time and place, because it can only be a danger to them. This scene can be played in various ways, but in our production it was very much this particular realisation of Juliet that was explored – it shows one of the ways in which she is pushed into a new responsibility and a new maturity.

Tybalt's death and Juliet's realisation of her total faith in Romeo serve as another step into a very different world; a world where she constantly has to find strength from within herself, a new strength which is fed by her love for Romeo. Both Romeo and Juliet are left on their own to deal with the hard realities of a threatening environment. Their only hope is the Friar's plot, and this too, fails them, and even he will desert Juliet at the very end because of his own fears. Not only does this rapidly bring changes to the outlook of these young people, but the quality of their love itself becomes more and more separated from the falsities and fallibilities of the real world – their love emerges more and more unique, more beautiful, timeless, and finally more tragic.

Their love gives them strength and courage to overcome their worst nightmares. Romeo is banished from his family, home and friends; Juliet rejects her family, submits to a magical potion and the horror of a catacomb. Finally they both overcome the ultimate test, and in their joint suicide it is the world that has lost, not the lovers, for Romeo and Juliet have the greater souls.

There is so very much to discover about the play and Juliet herself that I feel I have only skimmed the topmost surface here; one of the reasons I am so keen to play her again is because the discoveries within Shakespeare's characters are inexhaustible.

Juliet is an extraordinary person, susceptible to the most fearful premonitions, incredibly aware of human and earthly frailty and capable of the most enormous commitments of love. She is a unique individual – just as she becomes involved in a unique set of events. I adore the comedy of the balcony scene and Juliet's humour, her warmth and vulnerability, idiosyncrasies and impulsiveness, innate intelligence and insight, transformation from childhood into woman, relationship with the nurse, magnificent imagination and gift for expression, and finally her great, great love for her Romeo. Their love is both immediate and ultimate, and they cannot be parted even by death.

I have made no great reference here to the text as I feel that is another wonderful journey in itself. I have just tried to convey some of my feelings about the play and the part from a performer's point of view. Because I love both play and part passionately it is hard to feel I have done justice to either – so I will close with a few of Juliet's words, which I feel speak more volumes than I could ever write:

> My bounty is as boundless as the sea,
> My love as deep: the more I give to thee
> The more I have, for both are infinite.
> Act II Scene 2

Amanda Root
1989

Preface to this Edition

One of the guiding principles of this edition of *Romeo and Juliet* is that the student must have some idea of the play in performance and be able to produce it in his or her own mind before close study of the text is possible. A literary experience of a play is only valid after a theatrical one.

Some observations:

> Ideally, perhaps, the practical and critical study of a play should go hand in hand.
>
> *Drama: Education Survey 2* (HMSO, 1967, page 24)

> I assume that 'activities' . . . will take place. Study of this [critical] kind cannot be profitably undertaken without an approach through drama which includes improvisation and enactment. It also needs a varied approach through discussion which includes, for example, a forum in which critical viewpoints are presented and compared by pupil-advocates, who will learn in the process how to use the critics critically. And the approach through writing should include full-scale projects (if possible co-operatively prepared) as well as production notes for scenes and other variations on second-hand critical essays.
>
> Peter Hollindale, 'Approaches to Shakespeare at A-level' in *Teaching Shakespeare*, ed. Richard Adams (Robert Royce, London, 1985, page 95)

> The teacher could try to introduce the theatre into his classroom and his classroom to the theatre. The more this is done, the more the student is connected to the play as a vital thing.
>
> Braham Murray [Theatre Director], 'On Your Imaginary Forces Work' in *Teaching Shakespeare*, ed. Richard Adams (Robert Royce, London, 1985, page 56)

> This theatre is too easily a world of convention and ritual, where actors observe the picturesque decorum of Great Drama. The test is to make the world of the play answerable to the ordinary, commonsensical questions which audiences apply to the world outside it. Bogdanov describes directing a recent production of *Romeo and Juliet* at Stratford. "During the scene at the Capulet ball, Romeo sees Juliet and asks a servant who she is, and the servant replies, 'I know not'. Now why doesn't he know?" asks Bogdanov. "He works there and the party is being thrown in her honour. So has he just arrived or is he outside catering or what? It's one line, a small part, but that question is the key to acting that small part properly and therefore making the world of the play believable."
>
> Andrew Rissek, *The Independent*, 2 January 1987

> Mention has already been made of the value placed on the individual response. Sometimes examiners are faced with thirty or so answers that cover exactly the same ground in an almost identical way. Credit is given to these answers on their merits – they represent diligence on the part of teacher and taught, but they are at best competent and often rather flat; in other words, they are not likely to qualify for the highest marks because their imaginative content is so small. This really reinforces the point that candidates should be encouraged to come to terms with the text and to develop their own responses to it. Candidates who are drilled through the text line by line cannot be said to have experienced the most lively teaching, and their attitude to Shakespeare might well be adversely coloured by the experience. There are lively and inventive methods, many of them the subject of other parts of this book; all the evidence shows that such lively teaching in fact enhances the pass rates – it certainly makes for more enjoyable study.
>
> Ken Warren, 'Examining Shakespeare' in *Teaching Shakespeare*, ed. Richard Adams (Robert Royce, London, 1985, pages 148–9)

> One of my colleagues, who engages in as much scenic effect as possible when reading a Shakespeare play in class, has been known to bring in a forest of potted plants from his home in order to create a moving Birnam Wood - a great deal of fuss, of course, but his pupils will always remember that scene.
>
> Neil King, 'Starting Shakespeare' in *Teaching Shakespeare*, ed. Richard Adams (Robert Royce, London, 1985, page 67)

> To sum up: nothing is ephemeral in a performance text. An individual sitting in an audience watching the performance of a play is continually working at making a synthesis of the many and varied signals being transmitted by the actors, the setting, the costumes, the gestures, lighting properties, sound effects and so on. You cannot single out any one of these signal generators and give it priority over the rest. An active reader must be aware of the interconnection of everything that is seen and heard in performance.
>
> Peter Reynolds, *Drama: Text into Performance* (Penguin Masterstudies series, Harmondsworth, 1986, page 100)

> The notion of relevance has partly invaded all areas of modern life: things are only interesting in so far as they can be mapped onto current problems, current issues. . . .

> If you've got to make Shakespeare 'relevant', then junk it. It should be self-evidently relevant with a very short introduction. You shouldn't have to bend it into Belfast or Beirut to show that it's important. I think there are ways of showing it's interesting and relevant, even though it's in the past; perhaps *because* it's in the past. You don't have to go the lengths of putting it in leathers or on motorbikes, and that doesn't mean doing it in wrinkled tights either!
>
> Jonathan Miller in an interview with Rex Gibson, printed in *Shakespeare and Schools*, Newsletter 3, Summer 1987

This edition of *Romeo and Juliet* has been specifically designed with GCSE Literature in mind, but many of the activities will also provide useful material for GCSE English response to written material and, of course, oral work.

The marginal notes to the text provide enough glossary to enable the average student to work out what is going on in the text. Words whose meanings have not changed significantly have not been glossed; they can be looked up in a dictionary. Where possible, commentary has been replaced by questions in order to lead students towards an understanding, rather than telling them what to think (see, for example, the notes to Act II Scene 3 lines 63–4 on page 35). The emphasis is on encouraging students to think and draw conclusions for themselves.

This edition is not a mere crib, and is most useful when studied with the teacher. There are plenty of marginal suggestions and questions along the way and at the end of the book, but there is a deliberate omission of the kind of critical essay which weighs down students and leads them to think that any critical response must be written in a particular style. However, as well as the newer activity-based work, this edition provides much (traditional) literary stimulus which is useful for those who will go on to be students of A-level English. I hope that I have not annotated the play to death (as is the case with some editions currently available), but that one or two of the best tunes have been left for the teacher.

Neil King

Romeo and Juliet

List of characters

Escalus, Prince of Verona
Mercutio, a young gentleman and kinsman to the Prince, friend of Romeo
Paris, a noble young kinsman to the Prince
Page to Paris

Montague, head of a Veronese family at feud with the Capulets
Lady Montague
Romeo, Montague's son
Benvolio, Montague's nephew and friend of Romeo and Mercutio
Abram, a servant to Montague
Balthasar, Romeo's servant

Capulet, head of a Veronese family at feud with the Montagues
Lady Capulet
Juliet, Capulet's daughter
Tybalt, Lady Capulet's nephew
Capulet's **Cousin**, an old gentleman
Nurse, a Capulet servant, Juliet's foster-mother
Peter, a Capulet servant attending on the Nurse
Sampson
Gregory
Anthony } **Servants** of the Capulet household
Potpan

Friar Laurence
Friar John } of the Franciscan Order
An **Apothecary**, of Mantua
Three **Musicians** Simon Catling, Hugh Rebeck, James Soundpost
Watchmen, Citizens of Verona, Maskers, Torchbearers, Pages, Servants, Officers

The Scene: Verona and Mantua

Top and centre left and right:
Royal Shakespeare Company, 1976;
bottom: Royal Shakespeare Company, 1986

THE MOST EXCELLENT AND LAMENTABLE TRAGEDY OF ROMEO AND JULIET

The Prologue

[*Enter* **Chorus**]

Chorus   Two households both alike in dignity
(In fair Verona, where we lay our scene)
From ancient grudge break to new mutiny,
Where civil blood makes civil hands unclean.
From forth the fatal loins of these two foes   5
A pair of star-crossed lovers take their life,
Whose misadventured piteous overthrows
Doth with their death bury their parents' strife.
The fearful passage of their death-marked love
And the continuance of their parents' rage,   10
Which, but their children's end, nought could remove,
Is now the two hours' traffic of our stage;
The which, if you with patient ears attend,
What here shall miss, our toil shall strive to mend.   [*Exit*]

SD   **Chorus**   In the drama of ancient Greece, a number of people known as the chorus were used to comment on the main action of the play. Shakespeare uses a single actor as a chorus in several plays, and what he speaks here is in the form of a sonnet.
1   **both ... dignity**   both well-established families
2   **Verona**   an Italian town which Shakespeare also uses as a setting in *The Two Gentlemen of Verona* and *The Taming of the Shrew*
3   **break**   break out
mutiny   outbreak of violence
4   **civil blood**   the blood of civilians (as opposed to that of soliders)
6   **star-crossed**   ill-fated by the stars (referring to the belief, still held by many, that the stars determine people's destinies)
Look for further references to the influence of the stars as you work on the play.
7   **misadventured**   unfortunate
9   **passage**   voyage, course, channel
death-marked   marked out for death, as a navigation channel might be marked
The nautical image describes the lovers' voyage towards death.
11   **but**   except for
nought   nothing
12   **traffic**   activity, business
It is unlikely that the play took only two hours to perform. What impression do you think the Chorus is trying to give by this exaggeration?
14   **What here shall miss**   whatever is inadequate in our performance

Note: **SD** = stage direction

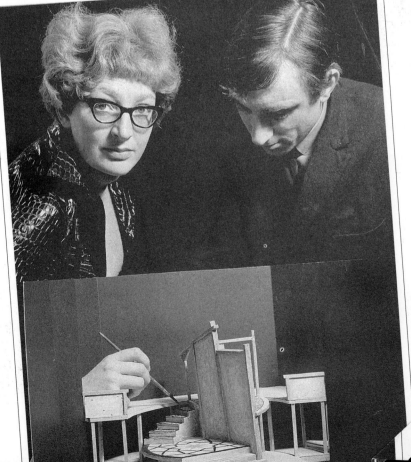

Designer at work on model for set of Bristol Old Vic production, 1966

SD *bucklers* small shields
1 **carry coals** that is, humiliated like the lowest servants (who performed tasks such as carrying coal)
3 **and** if
choler anger
draw that is, our swords
4 **collar** hangman's noose
Shakespeare and the Elizabethans loved this kind of punning (**colliers . . . choler . . . collar**), although sometimes, as here, the effect is rather forced. Dr Johnson, the great eighteenth-century critic, said that a pun was 'the fatal Cleopatra for which Shakespeare lost the world – and was content to lose it.'
5 **moved** aroused, made angry
The word carries the same meaning on lines 6 (**moved**) and 7 (**moves**), but **move** on line 8 means 'run away'. More punning from Gregory!
7 **dog** that is, a servant from the household (**house**) of Montague
Dogs were supposedly bad-tempered in hot weather. See Act III Scene 1 lines 23–5.
8 **stand** stand and fight
10 as in line 8, but with a sexual secondary meaning
11 **take the wall** The pavement nearest the wall is the best place to walk in order to avoid the mud and rubbish in the gutter. Sampson boasts that he will take the wall, implying that he will force any Montague whom he meets, man or woman, into the gutter.
12–13 **goes . . . wall** are pushed aside by the strong
15 **thrust to the wall** that is, in a sexual sense
In this exchange an image is created of crude animal behaviour in city and backstreets.
21 **civil** pleasant (he is being ironic, although possibly suggesting that taking maidenheads will be pleasant for him)
24 **maidenheads** virginity
25 **sense** meaning
26 **sense** feeling (a pun on the previous line)

Act I

Scene 1

A public place in Verona. Enter **Sampson** *and* **Gregory**, *with swords and bucklers, of the house of Capulet.*

Sampson   Gregory, on my word we'll not carry coals.

Gregory   No, for then we should be colliers.

Sampson   I mean, and we be in choler, we'll draw.

Gregory   Ay, while you live, draw your neck out of collar.

Sampson   I strike quickly being moved.   5

Gregory   But thou art not quickly moved to strike.

Sampson   A dog of the house of Montague moves me.

Gregory   To move is to stir, and to be valiant is to stand: therefore if thou art moved thou runn'st away.

Sampson   A dog of that house shall move me to stand. I will   10
take the wall of any man or maid of Montague's.

Gregory   That shows thee a weak slave, for the weakest goes to the wall.

Sampson   'Tis true, and therefore women, being the weaker vessels, are ever thrust to the wall; therefore I will push   15
Montague's men from the wall, and thrust his maids to the wall.

Gregory   The quarrel is between our masters and us their men.

Sampson   'Tis all one. I will show myself a tyrant: when I   20
have fought with the men I will be civil with the maids, I will cut off their heads.

Gregory   The heads of the maids?

Sampson   Ay, the heads of the maids, or their maidenheads;
take it in what sense thou wilt.   25

Gregory   They must take it in sense that feel it.

Set design for opening scene by Jean Hugo for Jean Cocteau's production, Paris, 1924

Sampson   Me they shall feel while I am able to stand, and 'tis known I am a pretty piece of flesh.

Gregory   'Tis well thou art not fish; if thou hadst, thou hadst been Poor John. Draw thy tool – here comes of the house of Montagues.   30

[*Enter two other* **Servants** (**Abram** *and* **Balthasar**)]

Sampson   My naked weapon is out. Quarrel, I will back thee.

Gregory   How, turn thy back and run?

Sampson   Fear me not.

Gregory   No, marry! I fear thee!   35

Sampson   Let us take the law of our sides: let them begin.

Gregory   I will frown as I pass by, and let them take it as they list.

Sampson   Nay, as they dare. I will bite my thumb at them, which is disgrace to them if they bear it.   40

Abram   Do you bite your thumb at us, sir?

Sampson   I do bite my thumb, sir.

Abram   Do you bite your thumb at us, sir?

Sampson   Is the law of our side if I say ay?

Gregory   No.   45

Sampson   No sir, I do not bite my thumb at you, sir, but I bite my thumb, sir.

Gregory   Do you quarrel, sir?

Abram   Quarrel, sir? No, sir.

Sampson   But if you do, sir, I am for you. I serve as good a man as you.   50

Abram   No better.

Sampson   Well, sir.

[*Enter* **Benvolio**]

27 **stand**   with sexual double-meaning
29 **fish**   (slang) prostitute
30 **Poor John**   dried hake, a poor quality fish
    tool   weapon (with obscene double-meaning)
    comes of   comes some of
32 **back thee**   back you up
34 **Fear me not**   that is, rely on me
35 another kind of punning
    Gregory pretends to take literally Sampson's **Fear me not**.
    marry   by (the Virgin) Mary – a common oath
36 **take . . . sides**   keep the law on our side
38 **list**   please
39 **bite my thumb**   an insulting gesture
40 **bear**   put up with, accept
44 **of**   on
50 **I am for you**   I'll take you on

> Consider how Sampson and Gregory talk together. Is this typical of the way in which young men still talk together?

54-5 Why do you think Gregory feels secure enough to be provocative?

59 washing swashing, slashing

60 up away

62 drawn that is, with your sword drawn
heartless hinds cowardly servants (with a pun on 'hinds' meaning female deer without a mate, and thus 'heartless')

63 In what way does Benvolio's name suggest the part he is to play?

68 Have at thee defend yourself (because I'm about to attack you)

69 bills and partisans spear-like weapons such as halberds and pikes

71 long sword a heavy old-fashioned weapon in Shakespeare's age (the light rapier was the modern weapon)
Why does Shakespeare include this detail?

72 What do you think Lady Capulet means by this line, and what does it tell us about (a) Capulet, (b) Lady Capulet?

74 spite scorn

What dramatic impression is created by Capulet rushing in wearing his nightgown?

Lines 69-78. Why should the director of the production shown below have decided to have Juliet present at this point in the play? Why in disguise? What is going on in the picture?

Temba Theatre Company 1988

Gregory   Say 'better', here comes one of my master's kinsmen.   55

Sampson   Yes, better, sir.

Abram   You lie.

Sampson   Draw if you be men. Gregory, remember thy washing blow.   *[They fight]*

Benvolio   Part, fools, put up your swords, you know not what   60
you do.

*[Enter **Tybalt**]*

Tybalt   What, art thou drawn among these heartless hinds? Turn thee, Benvolio, look upon thy death.

Benvolio   I do but keep the peace, put up thy sword, Or manage it to part these men with me.   65

Tybalt   What, drawn, and talk of peace? I hate the word, As I hate hell, all Montagues, and thee: Have at thee, coward.   *[They fight]*

*[Enter three or four **Citizens** with clubs or partisans]*

Citizens   Clubs, bills and partisans! Strike! Beat them down! Down with the Capulets! Down with the Montagues!   70

*[Enter old **Capulet** in his gown, and **Lady Capulet**]*

Capulet   What noise is this? Give me my long sword, ho!

Lady Capulet   A crutch, a crutch! Why call you for a sword?

*[Enter old **Montague** and **Lady Montague**]*

Capulet   My sword I say! Old Montague is come, And flourishes his blade in spite of me.

Montague   Thou villain Capulet! Hold me not! Let me go!   75

Lady Montague   Thou shalt not stir one foot to seek a foe.

[*Enter* **Prince Escalus** *with his* **Train**]

Prince   Rebellious subjects, enemies to peace,
    Profaners of this neighbour-stained steel –
    Will they not hear? What ho! You men, you beasts!
    That quench the fire of your pernicious rage   80
    With purple fountains issuing from your veins,
    On pain of torture from those bloody hands
    Throw your mistempered weapons to the ground
    And hear the sentence of your moved prince.
    Three civil brawls bred of an airy word   85
    By three, old Capulet, and Montague,
    Have thrice disturbed the quiet of our streets
    And made Verona's ancient citizens
    Cast by their grave-beseeming ornaments
    To wield old partisans, in hands as old,   90
    Cankered with peace, to part your cankered hate.
    If ever you disturb our streets again
    Your lives shall pay the forfeit of the peace.
    For this time all the rest depart away;
    You, Capulet, shall go along with me,   95
    And Montague, come you this afternoon,
    To know our farther pleasure in this case,
    To old Freetown, our common judgement-place.
    Once more, on pain of death, all men depart.

[*Exeunt (all but* **Montague**, **Lady Montague** *and* **Benvolio**)]

Montague   Who set this ancient quarrel new abroach?   100
    Speak, nephew, were you by when it began?

Benvolio   Here were the servants of your adversary
    And yours, close fighting ere I did approach.

78 **Profaners**   misusers, abusers
    neighbour-stained   This word is typical of
    Shakespeare's habit of coining new words by
    compounding old ones. What do you think he
    means here?
    steel   that is, swords
79 Describe what is happening on stage which
    prompts this line from the Prince. How should he
    deliver this line?
81 **purple . . . veins**   that is, blood
    Purple means dark red, rather than red and blue
    mixed.
83 **mistempered**   (i) badly tempered when made;
    (ii) used in bad temper by intemperate people
84 **sentence**   In what sense is the Prince using this
    word? Could the word bear more than one
    meaning?
    moved   See note to line 5.
85 **airy**   trivial, without substance
    word   remark, comment
    What else do we hear of the causes of the
    Capulet–Montague quarrel?
89 **by**   to one side
    grave-beseeming   suitably sober
91 **cankered . . . cankered**   grown rusty . . .
    cancerous
93 you will be executed as the penalty for breaking the
    peace
94 **this time**   now
97 **our farther pleasure**   our wishes in more detail
    (the Prince uses the royal plural)
99 **pain**   penalty
100 **abroach**   to pierce a barrel of liquor or gunpowder
    and leave it running
101 **by**   nearby
103 **ere**   before

Who set this ancient quarrel new abroach?
Speak, nephew, were you by when it began?

Albany Empire 1988

105 prepared   drawn ready for use
108 withal   at all
    In what tone does Benvolio talk of Tybalt's behaviour? See Mercutio's account, Act II Scene 4 lines 18–24.
110 part and part   some on one side, some on the other
111 either part   both sides
116 drive   drove
117 sycamore   a tree traditionally associated with love-sickness
    A pun on the name of the tree may have been intended. Can you think what it is?
118 westward . . . side   grows to the west on this side of the city
120 made   advanced
    ware   aware, wary
121 covert   concealment, cover
122 measuring his affections   judging his mood
124   that is, he is almost tired of his own company
125   followed my inclination (mood) by (i) not enquiring into his mood; (ii) not following him physically
126 who . . . from   one who was glad to avoid
128 augmenting   adding to
132 Aurora   In classical mythology Aurora, the goddess of the dawn, was supposed to leave the bed of Tithonus, her husband, each morning.
133 heavy   sad, but also possibly punning on the physical sense and playing on **light** earlier in the line
    son   Can you see how this word has also been chosen as a pun?
134 pens   shuts
137 portentous   evil-omened
    humour   It was supposed that a balance of four fluids or 'humours' in the body influenced mood. Montague fears that too much black bile is making Romeo melancholic.
138 counsel   advice

I drew to part them; in the instant came
The fiery Tybalt, with his sword prepared,   105
Which, as he breathed defiance to my ears
He swung about his head and cut the winds,
Who nothing hurt withal, hissed him in scorn.
While we were interchanging thrusts and blows
Came more and more, and fought on part and part,   110
Till the Prince came, who parted either part.

Lady Montague   O where is Romeo, saw you him today?
Right glad I am he was not at this fray.

Benvolio   Madam, an hour before the worshipped sun
Peered forth the golden window of the east   115
A troubled mind drive me to walk abroad,
Where underneath the grove of sycamore
That westward rooteth from this city side
So early walking did I see your son.
Towards him I made, but he was ware of me,   120
And stole into the covert of the wood.
I, measuring his affections by my own,
Which then most sought, where most might not be found,
Being one too many by my weary self,
Pursued my humour, not pursuing his,   125
And gladly shunned who gladly fled from me.

Montague   Many a morning hath he there been seen,
With tears augmenting the fresh morning's dew,
Adding to clouds more clouds with his deep sighs;
But all so soon as the all-cheering sun   130
Should in the farthest east begin to draw
The shady curtains from Aurora's bed,
Away from light steals home my heavy son
And private in his chamber pens himself,
Shuts up his windows, locks fair daylight out   135
And makes himself an artificial night.
Black and portentous must this humour prove
Unless good counsel may the cause remove.

Benvolio   My noble uncle, do you know the cause?

Montague   I neither know it nor can learn of him.   140

Re-read lines 77–155 of this scene. Consider (a) presentation of character, (b) dramatic interest and (c) poetic qualities in this section.

. . . early walking did I see your son.

Redgrave Theatre 1974

Benvolio   Have you importuned him by any means?

Montague   Both by myself and many other friends.
But he, his own affections' counsellor,
Is to himself – I will not say how true –
But to himself so secret and so close,   145
So far from sounding and discovery,
As is the bud bit with an envious worm
Ere he can spread his sweet leaves to the air
Or dedicate his beauty to the sun.
Could we learn from whence his sorrows grow,   150
We would as willingly give cure as know.

[*Enter* **Romeo**]

Benvolio   See where he comes. So please you step aside;
I'll know his grievance or be much denied.

Montague   I would thou wert so happy by thy stay
To hear true shrift. Come, madam, let's away.   155

[*Exeunt* **Montague** *and* **Lady Montague**]

Benvolio   Good morrow, cousin.

Romeo   Is the day so young?

Benvolio   But new struck nine.

Romeo   Ay me, sad hours seem long.
Was that my father that went hence so fast?

Benvolio   It was. What sadness lengthens Romeo's hours?

Romeo   Not having that which, having, makes them short.   160

Benvolio   In love?

Romeo   Out.

Benvolio   Of love?

Romeo   Out of her favour where I am in love.

Benvolio   Alas that love so gentle in his view   165
Should be so tyrannous and rough in proof.

Romeo   Alas that love whose view is muffled still
Should without eyes see pathways to his will.

141 **importuned** ques...
     any every
143 **his own affections'** ...
     seeking any advice from...
145 **close** secretive, uncomm...
146 **sounding and discovery**...
     depths discovered
     This is typical of the nautical im...
     Can you find other examples?
147 **with** by
     envious malicious
151 we are as eager to cure his sorrow as...
     what is upsetting him
152 **So please you** if you wouldn't mind
153 **grievance** what is making him melanchol...
     or . . . denied unless he is very stubborn in...
     resisting my questioning of him
154 **wert** were to be
155 **To hear true shrift** as to hear a true confession
     (of what is troubling Romeo)
157 **But new** only just
     It is clear that Romeo has been up for a long time.
     Why? Write a monologue which might have gone
     on in Romeo's head earlier that morning.
164 Romeo is referring to Rosaline, who is not
     mentioned by name until Act I Scene 2 line 85, and
     who does not appear in the play (unless a director
     wishes to make explicit her presence at Capulet's
     revels in Act I Scene 5).
165 **in his view** when viewed from a distance
166 **in proof** when it is actually experienced
167-8 Cupid, the little god of love, could always get his
     arrows to hit his target, even though he is
     considered to be blind (or at least blindfolded).

Costume design for Romeo
by Randolf Schwabe

Lyric Theatre 1919

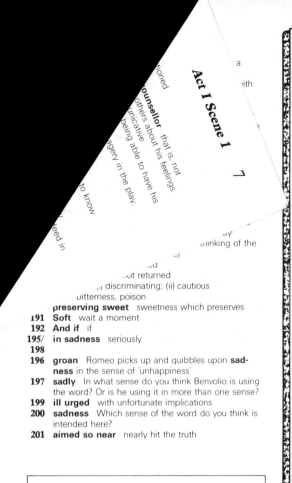

...tioned
...ounsellor that is, not
...others about his feelings
...unicative
...being able to have his
...agery in the play.

...to know

...eed in

...y
...inking of the

...returned
...discriminating; (ii) cautious
bitterness, poison
preserving sweet sweetness which preserves
191 **Soft** wait a moment
192 **And if** if
195/ **in sadness** seriously
198
196 **groan** Romeo picks up and quibbles upon **sadness** in the sense of 'unhappiness'
197 **sadly** In what sense do you think Benvolio is using the word? Or is he using it in more than one sense?
199 **ill urged** with unfortunate implications
200 **sadness** Which sense of the word do you think is intended here?
201 **aimed so near** nearly hit the truth

What do you think is Shakespeare's reason for showing Romeo already in love when the play opens?

Where shall we dine? O me! What fray was here?
Yet tell me not, for I have heard it all.   170
Here's much to do with hate, but more with love.
Why then, O brawling love, O loving hate,
O anything of nothing first create!
O heavy lightness, serious vanity,
Misshapen chaos of well-seeming forms!   175
Feather of lead, bright smoke, cold fire, sick health,
Still-waking sleep that is not what it is!
This love feel I that feel no love in this
Dost thou not laugh?

Benvolio   No coz, I rather weep.

Romeo   Good heart, at what?

Benvolio   At thy good heart's oppression.   180

Romeo   Why such is love's transgression.
Griefs of mine own lie heavy in my breast,
Which thou wilt propagate to have it pressed
With more of thine. This love that thou hast shown
Doth add more grief to too much of mine own.   185
Love is a smoke made with the fume of sighs;
Being purged, a fire sparkling in lovers' eyes;
Being vexed, a sea nourished with lovers' tears;
What is it else? A madness most discreet,
A choking gall, and a preserving sweet.   190
Farewell, my coz.

Benvolio   Soft, I will go along;
And if you leave me so, you do me wrong.

Romeo   Tut, I have lost myself, I am not here.
This is not Romeo, he's some other where.

Benvolio   Tell me in sadness who is that you love?   195

Romeo   What, shall I groan and tell thee?

Benvolio   Groan? Why no, but sadly tell me who.

Romeo   Bid a sick man in sadness make his will?
A word ill urged to one that is so ill.
In sadness, cousin, I do love a woman.   200

Benvolio   I aimed so near when I supposed you loved.

Tell me in sadness who is that you love?

Crucible Theatre 1984

Romeo   A right good mark-man; and she's fair I love.

Benvolio   A right fair mark, fair coz, is soonest hit.

Romeo   Well, in that hit you miss; she'll not be hit
With Cupid's arrow, she hath Dian's wit,   205
And in strong proof of chastity well armed
From love's weak childish bow she lives uncharmed.
She will not stay the siege of loving terms
Nor bide th'encounter of assailing eyes
Nor ope her lap to saint-seducing gold;   210
O she is rich in beauty, only poor
That when she dies, with beauty dies her store.

Benvolio   Then she hath sworn that she will still live chaste?

Romeo   She hath, and in that sparing makes huge waste.
For beauty starved with her severity   215
Cuts beauty off from all posterity.
She is too fair, too wise, wisely too fair,
To merit bliss by making me despair.
She hath forsworn to love, and in that vow
Do I live dead, that live to tell it now.   220

Benvolio   Be ruled by me, forget to think of her.

Romeo   O teach me how I should forget to think.

Benvolio   By giving liberty unto thine eyes:
Examine other beauties.

Romeo   'Tis the way
To call hers, exquisite, in question more.   225
These happy masks that kiss fair ladies' brows,
Being black, puts us in mind they hide the fair.
He that is strucken blind cannot forget
The precious treasure of his eyesight lost.
Show me a mistress that is passing fair;   230
What doth her beauty serve but as a note
Where I may read who passed that passing fair?
Farewell, thou canst not teach me to forget.

Benvolio   I'll pay that doctrine or else die in debt.

[*Exeunt*]

202 **mark-man** marksman
203 **right fair mark** good, clear target (with a pun
on **fair** meaning 'beautiful' in the previous line)
204 **hit . . . hit** aim, shot (that is, guess) . . . hit
205 **wit** wisdom (because Diana was the goddess of
chastity)
206 **proof** armour
207 What does this line mean? See the note to lines
167–8 if you need a clue.
208 **stay** wait and listen to (and so risk giving in to)
loving terms love talk
209 **bide** abide, put up with
210 nor let herself be seduced in return for gifts which
would corrupt a saint
212 **with . . . store** her supply (**store**) of beauty dies
with her (because she will leave no child)
This idea was popular in Elizabethan literature (see
Shakespeare's Sonnets 1–17 and *Twelfth Night*, Act
I Scene 5 lines 211–13). Which line on this page
repeats the idea?
213 **still live chaste** always remain a virgin
214 **sparing** economy (of her love)
215 **starved** that is, to death
218 **bliss** entry to heaven
despair that is, commit a deadly sin
219 **forsworn to** sworn not to
220 **live dead** live in a state as good as dead
224 **beauties** beautiful women
'Tis it is
225 to bring her exquisite beauty even more into my
thoughts
226 **masks** ladies sometimes wore black masks in
public
230 **passing** surpassingly, extremely
231 **note** that is, note in the margin (like this note!)
232 **passed** surpassed, exceeded

Temba Theatre Company 1988

1-3 In what tone do you think Capulet says these lines?
Is there hope of reconciliation here?

1 **bound**   bound over in legal obligation to keep the
peace

4 **reckoning**   reputation

6 **suit**   request for Juliet's hand in marriage

8 What does this line tell us about Juliet's upbringing?

9 **change**   that is, of seasons
fourteen   not considered in those days too young
to be a bride. In Shakespeare's *The Tempest*,
Miranda is fifteen.

13 **marred**   ruined, spoiled
Is there, perhaps, a pun intended here? Capulet
may be thinking that young mothers often died in
childbirth.

14 that is, all his other children are dead and buried
(and thus she is heir to the Capulet fortune)

15 all my hopes are centred upon her

16-19 How does Capulet's attitude here compare with his
later behaviour towards Juliet?

18 and once she has agreed, so long as (you are)
within the range of her choice

19 **fair according voice**   happy vote of agreement

20 **accustomed**   customary, traditional

22 **store**   company

25 mortal ladies who are like stars that reflect their
light back to heaven (which would otherwise be
dark)

26 **lusty**   vigorous

27 **well-apparelled**   that is, because dressed up in
new colours of leaves and flowers. See
Shakespeare's Sonnet 98, lines 2-3.

28 **limping**   that is, because winter departs slowly

29 **female buds**   girls about to open out into
womanhood

30 **Inherit**   become acquainted with

32 **of**   among, out of
mine   that is, my daughter

33 **in number**   among the general number (of ladies)
in reckoning none   in no way more special than
the others
Is Capulet's modesty sincere?

Scene 2

Verona. A street. Enter **Capulet, Paris** *and a* **Servant**.

Capulet   But Montague is bound as well as I,
In penalty alike, and 'tis not hard I think
For men so old as we to keep the peace.

Paris   Of honourable reckoning are you both,
And pity 'tis you lived at odds so long.   5
But now my lord, what say you to my suit?

Capulet   But saying o'er what I have said before.
My child is yet a stranger in the world,
She hath not seen the change of fourteen years.
Let two more summers wither in their pride   10
Ere we may think her ripe to be a bride.

Paris   Younger than she are happy mothers made.

Capulet   And too soon marred are those so early made.
Earth hath swallowed all my hopes but she;
She is the hopeful lady of my earth.   15
But woo her, gentle Paris, get her heart,
My will to her consent is but a part,
And she agreed, within her scope of choice
Lies my consent and fair according voice.
This night I hold an old accustomed feast   20
Whereto I have invited many a guest
Such as I love, and you among the store:
One more, most welcome, makes my number more.
At my poor house look to behold this night
Earth-treading stars that make dark heaven light.   25
Such comfort as do lusty young men feel
When well-apparelled April on the heel
Of limping winter treads, even such delight
Among fresh female buds shall you this night
Inherit at my house. Hear all, all see,   30
And like her most whose merit most shall be;
Which, on more view of many, mine, being one,
May stand in number, though in reckoning none.

Well-apparelled April

Woodcut by Roy Morgan

Come go with me. [*To* **Servant**] Go sirrah, trudge about
Through fair Verona, find those persons out   35
Whose names are written there, and to them say,
My house and welcome on their pleasure stay.

[*Exeunt* **Capulet** *and* **Paris**]

Servant   Find them out whose names are written here. It is
written that the shoemaker should meddle with his yard, and
the tailor with his last, the fisher with his pencil, and the   40
painter with his nets, but I am sent to find those persons
whose names are here writ, and can never find what names
the writing person hath here writ. I must to the learned. In
good time!

[*Enter* **Benvolio** *and* **Romeo**]

Benvolio   Tut man, one fire burns out another's burning,   45
   One pain is lessened by another's anguish;
   Turn giddy, and be holp by backward turning.
   One desperate grief cures with another's languish;
   Take thou some new infection to thy eye
   And the rank poison of the old will die.   50

Romeo   Your plaintain leaf is excellent for that.

Benvolio   For what, I pray thee?

Romeo   For your broken shin.

Benvolio   Why, Romeo, art thou mad?

Romeo   Not mad, but bound more than a madman is:
   Shut up in prison, kept without my food,   55
   Whipped and tormented and – good e'en, good fellow.

Servant   God gi' good e'en; I pray, sir, can you read?

Romeo   Ay, mine own fortune in my misery.

Servant   Perhaps you have learned it without book. But I pray
can you read anything you see?   60

Romeo   Ay, if I know the letters and the language.

Servant   Ye say honestly; rest you merry.

---

34   **sirrah**   fellow (used to address an inferior person such as a servant)
37   **on their pleasure stay**   are waiting (i) on their will to come; (ii) to give them pleasure
39–41   The servant mixes up the tradesmen and their tools. He is clearly not very bright!
39   **yard**   tailor's measure
43   **the learned**   that is, those who can read
43–4   **In good time!**   at just the right moment (here comes help)!
46   **another's anguish**   the hurt of another pain (not person)
47   **holp . . . turning**   helped by turning in the reverse direction
48   **cures . . . languish**   is cured by the pain caused by another grief
49   **infection**   The idea is of love as a sickness caught through the sight of the beloved.
50   **rank**   powerful
      old   old affection (that is, love)
51   The plaintain leaf was bound over minor injuries to prevent infection. Romeo is mocking Benvolio's comfort by pretending to take him seriously.
54–6   Romeo compares the afflictions of love with the treatment of the insane in Elizabethan times.
56   **e'en**   evening (used of any time after midday)
57   **God . . . e'en**   may God give you a good evening (or, simply, 'good evening')
58   **mine**   that is, I can read my
59   **without book**   by heart
62   **rest you merry**   may God give you happiness: (or, simply, 'goodbye')
      Why do you think the Servant starts to leave?

Re-read lines 45–50. The idea of a new pain which makes a person quite forget an old one is common. (See *Coriolanus*, Act IV Scene 7 line 54 and *King Lear*, Act III Scene 4 lines 8–9.) Talk or write about an occasion when this has happened to you.

It is a great coincidence that Romeo just happens to come across the Servant, and so finds out about the party which sets him towards his destiny. Look out for, and make a note of, other places in the play where chance is an important factor in the action.

I must to the learned.

Crucible Theatre 1984

65 County Count
70 Rosaline How would you advise the actor who plays Romeo to react to this name?
81-2 if . . . Montagues This is an example of dramatic irony, where the speaker is unaware of something of which the audience, and possibly other on-stage characters, are aware.
82 crush drink
To what do you think the 'crushing' refers, metaphorically speaking?
84 ancient meaning much the same as 'accustomed' at line 20
85 Rosaline Unless Romeo has made it clear at line 70, this is the first we know of the name of his love; for all we know at this point, his attentions could be directed towards the lady with whose name he is linked in the title of the play.
87 unattainted not infected; hence, unprejudiced
89 thy swan a crow because a swan is fair and a crow dark, and a fair complexion was considered desirable in Elizabethan times
Can you find other contrasts between light and darkness in the play?
90 The faith required in religion and in love were sometimes compared.
91 Maintains accepts
92 these that is, these eyes
drowned that is, with tears
93 Transparent obvious
Romeo refers to the testing of suspected witches by immersion in water, and to the burning of heretics who would not accept orthodox religious beliefs.
94-5 Look ahead and compare what Romeo says here with how he reacts when he first sees Juliet.

Re-read Benvolio's two speeches (lines 84–9 and 96–101). Find another place in Scene 2 where the same kind of advice is given.

What proportion of the play has passed before our first sight of Juliet? Is there a dramatic reason why Shakespeare withholds her for so long?

Romeo   Stay, fellow I can read.   [*He reads the letter*]
Signor Martino and his wife and daughters;
County Anselm and his beauteous sisters;   65
The lady widow of Utruvio;
Signor Placentio and his lovely nieces;
Mercutio and his brother Valentine;
Mine uncle Capulet, his wife and daughters;
My fair niece Rosaline and Livia;   70
Signor Valentio and his cousin Tybalt;
Lucio and the lively Helena.

A fair assembly. Whither should they come?

Servant   Up.

Romeo   Whither to supper?   75

Servant   To our house.

Romeo   Whose house?

Servant   My master's.

Romeo   Indeed I should have asked you that before.

Servant   Now I'll tell you without asking. My master is the   80
great rich Capulet, and if you be not of the house of
Montagues I pray come and crush a cup of wine. Rest you
merry.   [*Exit*]

Benvolio   At this same ancient feast of Capulet's
Sups the fair Rosaline, whom thou so loves,   85
With all the admired beauties of Verona.
Go thither and with unattainted eye
Compare her face with some that I shall show
And I will make thee think thy swan a crow.

Romeo   When the devout religion of mine eye   90
Maintains such falsehood, then turn tears to fire,
And these who, often drowned, could never die,
Transparent heretics, be burnt for liars.
One fairer than my love! The all-seeing sun
Ne'er saw her match since first the world begun.   95

Benvolio   Tut, you saw her fair, none else being by:
Herself poised with herself in either eye.

God's all-seeing eye represented as the sun. The sun was sometimes seen as the eye of God, which saw everything. In this woodcut a sinner is trying to hide from God's all-seeing eye (Ubies = Everywhere).

Woodcut from Geoffrey Whitney, *A Choice of Emblemes*, 1586

But in that crystal scales let there be weighed
Your lady's love against some other maid
That I will show you shining at this feast,   100
And she shall scant show well that now seems best.

Romeo   I'll go along, no such sight to be shown,
But to rejoice in splendour of mine own.   [*Exeunt*]

Scene 3

A room in Capulet's house. Enter **Lady Capulet** *and* **Nurse**.

Lady Capulet   Nurse, where's my daughter? Call her forth to
me.

Nurse   Now by my maidenhead at twelve year old, I bade her
come. What, lamb! What, ladybird! God forbid! Where's this
girl? What, Juliet!

[*Enter* **Juliet**]

Juliet   How now, who calls?

Nurse   Your mother.   5

Juliet   Madam, I am here, what is your will?

Lady Capulet   This is the matter. Nurse, give leave awhile,
We must talk in secret. Nurse, come back again,
I have remembered me, thou's hear our counsel.
Thou knowest my daughter's of a pretty age.   10

Nurse   Faith, I can tell her age unto an hour.

Lady Capulet   She's not fourteen.

Nurse   I'll lay fourteen of my teeth –
and yet, to my teen be it spoken, I have but four – she's not
fourteen. How long is it now to Lammas-tide?   15

Lady Capulet   A fortnight and odd days.

Nurse   Even or odd, of all days in the year, come Lammas
Eve at night shall she be fourteen. Susan and she – God rest

97-9 The image is that of a pair of scales, with Romeo's
two eyes as the two pans of the balance (**crystal
scales**). At present Rosaline is weighed (**poised**) by
both of Romeo's eyes; Benvolio urges that she be
weighed against the sight of some other girl. Do
you think this imagery is successful?
101 **scant** scarcely
103 **mine own** that is, his own love Rosaline
(In view of his reason for going to the party, the
outcome will prove to be very ironic.)

2 **maidenhead ... old** the inference is that she lost
her virginity soon afterwards
3 **What** a word often used to show impatience
7 **matter** business
give leave leave us for
9 **thou's** thou shalt, you must
10 **pretty** marriageable
13 **teen** sadness (note the play on words)
15 **Lammas-tide** 1st August, traditionally a day for
celebrating the first fruits of harvest
16-17 What do you think Lady Capulet means by **odd**,
and how does the Nurse misunderstand her?

Costume design for Lady Capulet
by Jean Hugo for Jean Cocteau's
production, Paris, 1924

19 Susan It is to be presumed that this is the Nurse's daughter who was born at the same time as Juliet (they were **of an age**), and whose infant death enabled the Nurse to wet-nurse Juliet.
21 marry by Mary (a mild oath)
24 wormwood a bitter oil which was rubbed onto the nipple in order to wean babies off the breast (**dug**)
26 Mantua a town near Verona, where Romeo seeks refuge later in the play
       bear a brain have a good memory (Has she?)
27 it that is, baby Juliet
28 fool used here as a term of affection
       See *King Lear*, Act V Scene 3 line 306.
       tetchy irritable
29 'Shake!' ... dove-house a fanciful way of saying that the dove-house shook in the earthquake
       no need that is, she did not need to be told twice
30 bid me trudge tell me to be off
31 high-lone upright by herself (without support)
       rood Christ's cross
33 broke her brow cut or bruised her forehead
34 'A he
35–6 fall backward that is, underneath a lover
36 wit understanding
37 holidame holiness; but often ignorantly supposed, as here by the Nurse, to mean 'holy dame' – that is, the Virgin Mary
38 come about become reality (because Juliet is now of marriageable age)
       and if
40 fool See note to line 28.
       it stinted she ceased (crying)
45 it ... it the baby ... its ('its' was rarely used in Shakespeare's day)
46 stone testicle
       perilous nasty
50 Can you spot the pun in this line? How do you think the actress playing Juliet should react to the Nurse's story?
51 mark ... grace that is, save your soul
53 once some day

What age do you suppose the Nurse to be? Is there any evidence in this scene?

What kind of a character do you imagine the Nurse's husband to have been? Write a short dramatic fragment depicting the scene which the Nurse is recalling.

Peace, I have done.

Compass Theatre Company 1987–8

Compass are a small-scale touring company with half-a-dozen actors. 'Doubling-up' means that sometimes men have to play women's parts and vice-versa. Elizabethan touring companies, which usually consisted of about five men and a boy (to play the female roles), understood this constraint only too well.

---

all Christian souls – were of an age. Well, Susan is with God; she was too good for me. But as I said, on Lammas Eve at night shall she be fourteen. That shall she; marry, I remember it well. 'Tis since the earthquake now eleven years, and she was weaned – I never shall forget it – of all the days of the year upon that day. For I had then laid wormwood to my dug, sitting in the sun under the dovehouse wall. My lord and you were then at Mantua – nay I do bear a brain! But as I said, when it did taste the wormwood on the nipple of my dug and felt it bitter, pretty fool, to see it tetchy and fall out with the dug. 'Shake!' quoth the dove-house. 'Twas no need, I trow, to bid me trudge. And since that time it is eleven years. For then she could stand high-lone, nay, by th'rood, she could have run and waddled all about; for even the day before she broke her brow, and then my husband – God be with his soul, 'a was a merry man – took up the child, 'Yea', quoth he, 'dost thou fall upon thy face? Thou wilt fall backward when thou hast more wit, wilt thou not, Jule?' And by my holidame, the pretty wretch left crying and said 'Ay'. To see now how a jest shall come about. I warrant, and I should live a thousand years I never should forget it. 'Wilt thou not, Jule?' quoth he, and, pretty fool, it stinted, and said 'Ay'.   20

25

30

35

40

Lady Capulet   Enough of this, I pray thee, hold thy peace.

Nurse   Yes, madam. [*She pauses*] Yet I cannot choose but laugh to think it should leave crying and say 'Ay'; and yet I warrant it had upon it brow a bump as big as a young cockerel's stone, a perilous knock, and it cried bitterly. 'Yea', quoth my husband, 'fall'st upon thy face? Thou wilt fall backward when thou comest to age, wilt thou not, Jule?' It stinted, and said 'Ay'.   45

Juliet   And stint thou too, I pray thee, Nurse, say I.   50

Nurse   Peace, I have done. God mark thee to his grace, thou wast the prettiest babe that e'er I nursed. And I might live to see thee married once, I have my wish.

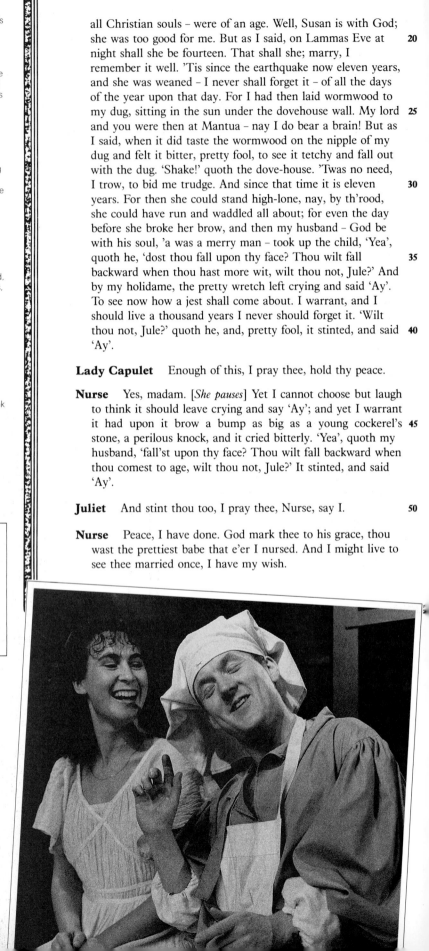

Lady Capulet   Marry, that marry is the very theme
I came to talk of. Tell me, daughter Juliet,   **55**
How stands your dispositions to be married?

Juliet   It is an honour that I dream not of.

Nurse   An honour. Were not I thine only nurse I would say
thou hadst sucked wisdom from thy teat.

Lady Capulet   Well, think of marriage now. Younger than you   **60**
Here in Verona, ladies of esteem,
Are made already mothers. But my count
I was your mother much upon these years
That you are now a maid. Thus then in brief:
The valiant Paris seeks you for his love.   **65**

Nurse   A man, young lady. Lady, such a man as all the
world – why, he's a man of wax.

Lady Capulet   Verona's summer hath not such a flower.

Nurse   Nay, he's a flower, in faith a very flower.

Lady Capulet   What say you, can you love the gentleman?   **70**
This night you shall behold him at our feast;
Read o'er the volume of young Paris' face
And find delight writ there with beauty's pen.
Examine every married lineament
And see how one another lends content;   **75**
And what obscured in this fair volume lies,
Find written in the margent of his eyes.
This precious book of love, this unbound lover,
To beautify him only lacks a cover.
The fish lives in the sea; and 'tis much pride   **80**
For fair without the fair within to hide.
That book in many's eyes doth share the glory
That in gold clasps locks in the golden story.
So shall you share all that he doth possess,
By having him, making yourself no less.   **85**

Nurse   No less, nay bigger. Women grow by men.

Lady Capulet   Speak briefly, can you like of Paris' love?

56 How do you feel disposed towards being married?
59 **thy** that is, from my nipple
62 **count** calculation (with a bawdy double-meaning)
63 **much upon these years** at about the same age
67 **of wax** that is, like a faultless model
72–83 In an extended metaphor, Lady Capulet compares Paris with an expensive manuscript book. Do you think that this is an effective piece of writing, or is it rather forced?
73 **delight** a delightful prospect
74 **married lineament** harmoniously blended feature
75 **one . . . content** each part enhances another
76 and what cannot easily be detected in his face
77 **margent** margin, where explanatory notes often appear in books (as here!) See *Hamlet*, Act V Scene 2 lines 155-6.
78 **unbound** unmarried (punning upon marriage and the binding of a book as both tying together)
79 **a cover** that is (i) of a book; (ii) the embrace of a wife
80–1 No satisfactory explanation for these lines has ever been suggested. Can you offer one?
82–3 Juliet is the binding of the book which will share in the honour given to the content (that is, Paris). What may the **gold clasps** of the book also be taken as a symbol of?
86 **grow** because they become pregnant In what way is this interruption typical of the Nurse?
87 **like of** take pleasure in

Lyceum Theatre 1882

88 I'll expect to like him, if looking at him leads me to like him
89 **endart** pierce like a dart or arrow
89–90 but I will not let myself fall further in love than you consent to
The image is that of one of Cupid's arrows flying to its mark. It is ironic that by the next day Juliet has fallen in love and married without her parents' knowledge or consent.
92–3 **in the pantry** Why do you suppose that the Nurse is cursed in the pantry? See Act IV Scene 4 line 5.
93 **in extremity** in need of urgent attention
94 **straight** straightaway, immediately
95 **stays** is waiting (for you)
96 **to** after
As usual, the Nurse slips in a sexual innuendo.

What is the effect of the entry of the Servant and his outburst of vigorous prose after the previous speeches in verse?

1–2 It was customary for gatecrashers to deliver a speech to explain their presence. The host normally regarded such an intrusion as a compliment. (See Capulet's reaction to Romeo's presence in the next scene.)
3 such tedious apologies are out-of-date
4 **Cupid** maskers were usually introduced by the figure of Cupid
hoodwinked blindfolded
5 **Tartar's painted bow** a bow shaped like an upper lip and traditionally carried by Cupid
lath thin wood
6 **crowkeeper** scarecrow, or a boy hired to scare crows
7 **without-book** memorised
spoke spoken
8 **After** assisted by
What is the function of a prompter in the theatre?
9 **measure** judge
what they will whatever standards they desire
10 **measure . . . measure** have a dance with them (that is, the ladies)
11 **torch** by carrying a torch he would become an observer, and not take part in the masked dance
ambling dancing
In what tone do you think Romeo should say this word?
12 **heavy** See Act I Scene 1 line 182.
15 **soles . . . soul** Explain this typically Shakespearean pun (see *Julius Caesar*, Act I Scene 1 line 19).
16 The image is from bear-baiting, where bears were chained to a heavy stake and attacked by dogs. The bear-baiting pit was situated within earshot of the Globe Theatre, and there are many metaphors taken from bear-baiting in Shakespeare's plays (see, for instance, *Macbeth*, Act III Scene 4 line 101 and Act V Scene 7 line 1, and *King Lear*, Act III Scene 7 line 54).

Juliet   I'll look to like, if looking liking move,
But no more deep will I endart mine eye
Than your consent gives strength to make it fly.   90

[*Enter a* **Servant**]

Servant   Madam, the guests are come, supper served up, you called, my young lady asked for, the Nurse cursed in the pantry, and everything in extremity. I must hence to wait, I beseech you follow straight.   [*Exit*]

Lady Capulet   We follow thee; Juliet, the County stays.   95

Nurse   Go, girl, seek happy nights to happy days.   [*Exeunt*]

Scene 4

Enter **Romeo**, **Mercutio**, **Benvolio**, *with five or six other* **Maskers** *and* **Torchbearers**.

Benvolio   What, shall this speech be spoke for our excuse?
Or shall we on without apology?

Mercutio   The date is out of such prolixity.
We'll have no Cupid hoodwinked with a scarf,
Bearing a Tartar's painted bow of lath,   5
Scaring the ladies like a crowkeeper,
Nor no without-book prologue, faintly spoke
After the prompter, for our entrance.
But let them measure us by what they will,
We'll measure them a measure and be gone.   10

Romeo   Give me a torch, I am not for this ambling.
Being but heavy I will bear the light.

Mercutio   Nay, gentle Romeo, we must have you dance.

Romeo   Not I, believe me. You have dancing shoes
With nimble soles, I have a soul of lead   15
So stakes me to the ground I cannot move.

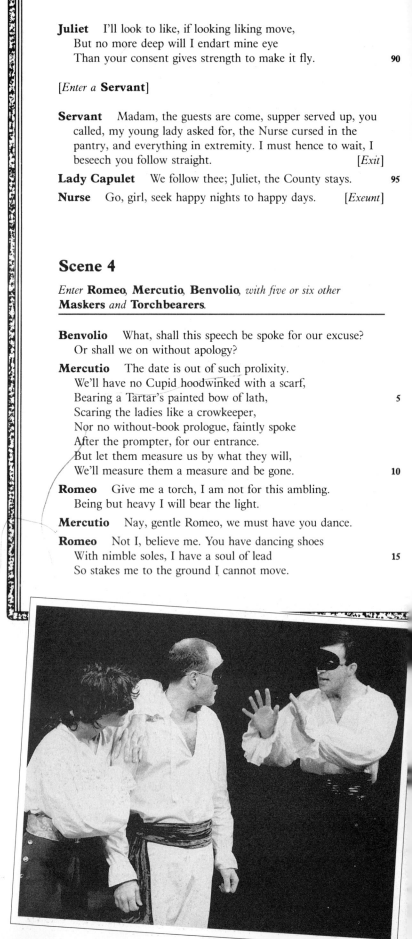

. . . gentle Romeo, we must have you dance.

Compass Theatre Company 1987–8

Mercutio   You are a lover, borrow Cupid's wings
And soar with them above a common bound.

Romeo   I am too sore enpiercèd with his shaft
To soar with his light feathers, and so bound   20
I cannot bound a pitch above dull woe.
Under love's heavy burden do I sink.

Mercutio   And, to sink in it, should you burden love –
Too great oppression for a tender thing.

Romeo   Is love a tender thing? It is too rough,   25
Too rude, too boisterous, and it pricks like thorn.

Mercutio   If love be rough with you, be rough with love;
Prick love for pricking and you beat love down.
Give me a case to put my visage in:
A visor for a visor. What care I   30
What curious eye doth quote deformities?
Here are the beetle brows shall blush for me.

Benvolio   Come, knock and enter, and no sooner in
But every man betake him to his legs.

Romeo   A torch for me. Let wantons light of heart   35
Tickle the senseless rushes with their heels,
For I am proverbed with a grandsire phrase –
I'll be a candle-holder and look on.
The game was ne'er so fair, and I am done.

Mercutio   Tut, dun's the mouse, the constable's own word.   40
If thou art Dun, we'll draw thee from the mire
Of – save your reverence – love, wherein thou stickest
Up to the ears. Come, we burn daylight, ho.

Romeo   Nay, that's not so.

Mercutio   I mean sir, in delay
We waste our lights in vain, like lamps by day.   45
Take our good meaning, for our judgement sits
Five times in that ere once in our five wits.

Romeo   And we mean well in going to this mask,
But 'tis no wit to go.

18   **bound** (i) limit; (ii) leap in dancing
(Some dancing of the time required high leaps or
'capers' in the air.)
19   **sore enpiercèd**   badly wounded
20   **bound**   tied down
21   **pitch**   the height from which a falcon swoops to kill
23   Mercutio says that in order to make love it is
necessary to be a weight upon the woman he loves.
26   It was supposed that a nightingale sang its love-song
while pricking its breast upon a thorn. (There are
obvious bawdy puns here and elsewhere in this section.)
28   **for pricking**   for giving you pain
29   **case**   mask
        visage   face
30   **visor . . . visor**   mask for an ugly face
31   **quote deformities**   observe (my) ugliness
32   It seems that Mercutio's mask has bushy eyebrows
and red cheeks.
34   **betake . . . legs**   What does Benvolio mean by this?
35   **wantons**   merrymakers
35–6   How would you describe Romeo's attitude towards
the **wantons**?
36   **senseless**   incapable of feeling
Rushes were laid upon the floors of Elizabethan
houses, and possibly the stage also.
37   **proverbed . . . phrase**   supported by an old
proverb (that the onlooker – that is, the candle-
holder – sees the best of the game)
39   Possibly referring to the proverb that when the
game is at its best, it is time to leave; but the
meaning of the line is uncertain.
40   **dun's the mouse**   be quiet
Can you think of two reasons why a brown (**dun**)
mouse may be proverbial for keeping quiet?
        constable's own word   that is, what the
constable says when he wishes to be quiet in order
to catch a criminal
41   **Dun**   common name for a horse
        mire   mud, in which horses sometimes got stuck
What name do we sometimes give to one who will
not get up and enjoy himself? 'Dun in the mire' was
also a Christmas game in which a heavy log had to
be lifted.
42   **save your reverence**   begging your pardon
43   **burn daylight**   In what metaphorical sense do you
think Mercutio means this? (In the next line Romeo
takes him literally, or pretends to.) Look ahead to
lines 44–7.
46   **good**   general
Mercutio means that his overall sense is five times
more significant than what can be gathered
through any one of our five senses.
49   **'tis no wit**   it is unwise

The original manuscript assigns lines 1–2 to
Romeo, and lines 3–10 to Benvolio, and
most editors go along with this. From their
content, can you support the case for the
changes made by the editor of this edition?

What kind of character is suggested by
Mercutio's name? (Look up 'mercurial' in the
dictionary.) Suggest what first impressions
the actor playing the role should attempt to
make upon the audience.

                . . . borrow Cupid's wings
And soar with them above a common bound.

Young Vic 1987–8

50 tonight last night
53 Queen Mab the Fairy Queen (it is possible that her name comes from Celtic mythology)
54 midwife because she delivers dreams and fantasies to sleepers
55 agate semi-precious stone carved and set in signet rings
57 atomies creatures as tiny as atoms
60 The sharp tooth of the squirrel and of the hole-boring grub make them useful in fairy joinery.
61 Time out o' mind from time immemorial
62 spinners spiders or, possibly, daddy-longlegs
64 traces reins
67 waggoner driver
69 lazy . . . maid It was believed that tiny insects bred in the hands of idle maidens.
70 state stately progress
72 curtsies bowings and other signs of respect
straight immediately
78 suit court case
79 tithe-pig A parson was entitled to one pig in ten in his parish. Look up 'tithe' in a dictionary.
80 'a he
81 benefice living
Parsons sometimes abused the system by receiving incomes from several churches.

Albany Empire 1988

Mercutio	Why, may one ask?
Romeo	I dreamt a dream tonight.
Mercutio	And so did I. 50
Romeo	Well what was yours?
Mercutio	That dreamers often lie.
Romeo	In bed asleep, while they do dream things true.

Mercutio   O then I see Queen Mab hath been with you.
She is the fairies' midwife, and she comes
In shape no bigger than an agate stone   55
On the forefinger of an alderman,
Drawn with a team of little atomies
Over men's noses as they lie asleep.
Her chariot is an empty hazelnut
Made by the joiner squirrel or old grub,   60
Time out o' mind the fairies' coachmakers;
Her waggon-spokes made of long spinners' legs,
The cover of the wings of grasshoppers,
Her traces of the smallest spider web,
Her collars of the moonshine's watery beams,   65
Her whip of cricket's bone, the lash of film,
Her waggoner a small grey-coated gnat,
Not half so big as a round little worm
Pricked from the lazy finger of a maid;
And in this state she gallops night by night   70
Through lovers' brains, and then they dream of love;
O'er courtiers' knees, that dream on curtsies straight;
O'er lawyers' fingers who straight dream on fees;
O'er ladies' lips, who straight on kisses dream,
Which oft the angry Mab with blisters plagues   75
Because their breaths with sweetmeats tainted are.
Sometime she gallops o'er a counsellor's nose
And then dreams he of smelling out a suit;
And sometime comes she with a tithe-pig's tail,
Tickling a parson's nose as 'a lies asleep;   80
Then dreams he of another benefice.
Sometimes she driveth o'er a soldier's neck

The River Thames was the main artery of a city which was increasingly becoming a sea-going port, and images of boats and ships were an everyday occurrence for the Elizabethan Londoner. See lines 112–13 opposite.

And then dreams he of cutting foreign throats,
Of breaches, ambuscados, Spanish blades,
Of healths five fathom deep; and then anon   85
Drums in his ear, at which he starts and wakes,
And being thus frighted, swears a prayer or two
And sleeps again. This is that very Mab
That plaits the manes of horses in the night
And bakes the elf-locks in foul sluttish hairs,   90
Which, once untangled, much misfortune bodes.
This is the hag, when maids lie on their backs,
That presses them and learns them first to bear,
Making them women of good carriage.
This is she –

Romeo   Peace, peace, Mercutio, peace.   95
Thou talk'st of nothing.

Mercutio   True, I talk of dreams,
Which are the children of an idle brain,
Begot of nothing but vain fantasy,
Which is as thin of substance as the air
And more inconstant than the wind, who woos   100
Even now the frozen bosom of the north
And, being angered, puffs away from thence
Turning his side to the dew-dropping south.

Benvolio   This wind you talk of blows us from ourselves:
Supper is done and we shall come too late.   105

Romeo   I fear too early, for my mind misgives
Some consequence yet hanging in the stars
Shall bitterly begin his fearful date
With this night's revels, and expire the term
Of a despised life closed in my breast   110
By some vile forfeit of untimely death.
But He that hath the steerage of my course
Direct my sail! On, lusty gentlemen!

Benvolio   Strike, drum.   [*They march about the stage*]

84 **breaches** that is, in a defensive wall
       ambuscados ambushes
       Spanish blades Toledo steel was famous for its
       quality.
85 **healths . . . deep** heavy drinking
       anon immediately
89–90 It was believed that elves were responsible for
       matted hair in horses and in dirty humans.
91 **untangled** entangled (that is, tangled)
92–4 It was thought that an evil spirit (**hag**) could
       produce nightmares and erotic dreams, and
       descend upon sleeping maids and make them
       pregnant.
93 **bear** carry (i) the weight of a lover; (ii) children
94 **carriage** (i) bearing children; (ii) deportment;
       (iii) bearing of a lover's weight
104 **ourselves** our intentions (to go to the party)
106– Perhaps Romeo's premonition has something to do
11 with his dream, referred to back at line 50. What
       do you think?
109 **expire the term** a legal phrase implying that, if a
       mortgage is not paid by a given date, a penalty
       (**forfeit**) must be paid (in this case, Romeo's life)
112 **He** God

On, lusty gentlemen!

Bristol Old Vic 1959

1 **take** clear
2 **trencher** wooden plate
5 **joint-stools** wooden stools fitted together by a joiner
5–6 **court-cupboard** sideboard
6 **look to the plate** take care of the tableware (of silver or pewter, which might be displayed on the sideboard)
  Good thou my good fellow
7 **marchpane** marzipan
11 **the great chamber** the hall of a big house
13 **longer . . . all** that is, enjoy yourself while you can (for Death will claim you in the end)
14 **Welcome** whom is the hospitable Capulet addressing?
15 **walk a bout** have a dance
17 **deny** refuse
  makes dainty hesitates
18 **Am . . . ye** Have I hit on the truth? In what tone do you think Capulet should say this?
24 **A hall, a hall!** He is calling for the clearing of a space for dancing in the hall.

> Who is Potpan, do you think? What is the first and second Servants' attitude towards him? Whom do you suppose are Susan and Nell, and why are they coming?

Scene 5

The hall in Capulet's house. **Servants** *enter with napkins.*

1st Servant Where's Potpan that he helps not to take away? He shift a trencher! He scrape a trencher!

2nd Servant When good manners shall lie all in one or two men's hands, and they unwashed too, 'tis a foul thing.

1st Servant Away with the joint-stools, remove the court-cupboard, look to the plate. Good thou, save me a piece of marchpane, and as thou loves me, let the porter let in Susan Grindstone and Nell – Anthony, and Potpan!   5

3rd Servant Ay boy, ready.

1st Servant You are looked for and called for, asked for and sought for, in the great chamber.   10

4th Servant We cannot be here and there too. Cheerly, boys! Be brisk awhile, and the longer liver take all.

[*Exeunt* **Servants**]

[*Enter* **Capulet, Lady Capulet, Juliet, Tybalt, Nurse** *and all the* **Guests** *and* **Gentlewomen** *to the* **Maskers**]

Capulet Welcome, gentlemen, ladies that have their toes
Unplagued with corns will walk a bout with you.   15
Ah my mistresses, which of you all
Will now deny to dance? She that makes dainty,
She I'll swear hath corns. Am I come near ye now?
Welcome, gentlemen. I have seen the day
That I have worn a visor and could tell   20
A whispering tale in a fair lady's ear,
Such as would please. 'Tis gone, 'tis gone, 'tis gone,
You are welcome, gentlemen: come, musicians, play.
A hall, a hall! Give room! And foot it girls!

[*Music plays and they dance*]

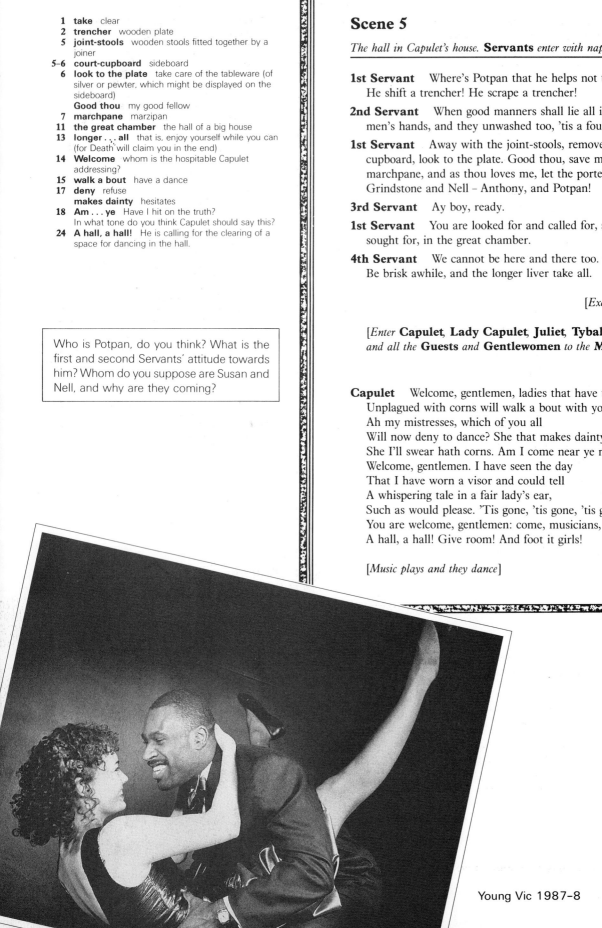

Young Vic 1987–8

More light, you knaves, and turn the tables up. 25
And quench the fire, the room is grown too hot.
Ah sirrah, this unlooked-for sport comes well.
Nay sit, nay sit, good cousin Capulet,
For you and I are past our dancing days.
How long is't now since last yourself and I 30
Were in a mask?

Cousin Capulet   By'r Lady, thirty years.

Capulet   What, man, 'tis not so much, 'tis not so much.
'Tis since the nuptial of Lucentio,
Come Pentecost as quickly as it will,
Some five and twenty years: and then we masked. 35

Cousin Capulet   'Tis more, 'tis more, his son is elder, sir:
His son is thirty.

Capulet   Will you tell me that?
His son was but a ward two years ago.

Romeo   What lady's that which doth enrich the hand
Of yonder knight?

Servant   I know not, sir. 40

Romeo   O, she doth teach the torches to burn bright.
It seems she hangs upon the cheek of night
As a rich jewel in an Ethiop's ear –
Beauty too rich for use, for earth too dear.
So shows a snowy dove trooping with crows 45
As yonder lady o'er her fellows shows.
The measure done, I'll watch her place of stand,
And touching hers, make blessed my rude hand.
Did my heart love till now? Forswear it, sight.
For I ne'er saw true beauty till this night. 50

Tybalt   This by his voice should be a Montague.
Fetch me my rapier, boy. [*Exit* **Boy**] What, dares the slave
Come hither, covered with an antic face,
To fleer and scorn at our solemnity?
Now by the stock and honour of my kin, 55
To strike him dead I hold it not a sin.

Capulet   Why how now, kinsman, wherefore storm you so?

25   turn
     and p
27   sirra
     Cap
     Wh
     a p
31   W
     m

33
34
3t

     under t.
     After Capulet s t.
     see and hear?
43   **Ethiop**   Ethiopian, but in Elizabeth.
     any black African
44   **use**   the use of this word
     dear   valuable
45   **trooping with**   amongst
     See Act I Scene 2 line 89.
46   **o'er...shows**   appears above her female
     companions
47   **measure**   dance
     of stand   where she goes to stand
48   **rude**   coarse, presumptuous
     Romeo is regarding Juliet as he might the statue of
     a saint.
49   **Forswear**   break off (his oath to Rosaline)
49–50   Search back in the text and discover what is ironic
     in these lines in view of Benvolio's comments earlier
     in the Act.
51   **should**   must
52   **What**   how
53   **antic face**   carnival mask (such masks were often
     comic or grotesque)
54   **fleer**   From the sound and context of this word,
     can you guess what it means?
     solemnity   festive celebration
55   **stock**   family

61   Does Capulet alread.
62   **Content thee**   c
     contented state   c
     coz   kinsman   c
     times could   h
     portly   well-ç
     report)   w
63   **well-ç   disp
65   be
67
68
69

Spot images of light and darkness on this
page.

There are several rhyming couplets on this
page. Is there any effect created by them?

How does Capulet present himself in this
scene? What values does he hold dear?
Refer to details to justify what you say.

Why how now, kinsman, wherefore storm you so?

Redgrave Theatre 1974

... know, perhaps?
... alm down, keep yourself in a
... of mind
... (from 'cousin', which in Elizabethan
... e used of any close relation)
... ll-mannered, dignified (literally, of good

... **overned** of responsible behaviour
... **aragement** an indignity
... **patient** accept it calmly
... **ote** notice
Capulet's tone seems to change here. What do you
think the actor playing Tybalt should do to provoke
this?

70 **fair presence** cheerful behaviour
71 **ill-beseeming semblance** unsuitable facial
expression
74 **goodman** that is, insolent; 'goodman' was a rank
below 'gentleman', and is here used of one not
behaving like a gentleman
Go to! an expression of impatience
76 **God . . . soul** equivalent to 'Bless me' or 'God give
me strength'
77 **mutiny** disturbance
78 **set cock-a-hoop** run riot
you'll be the man! you must play the boss
80 **saucy** insolent (used more strongly than in
modern English)
See Act II Scene 4 line 130.
81 **trick** behaviour (in this case, aggressiveness)
scathe injure
Capulet may be hinting at punishing him financially;
but it is ironic that Tybalt's behaviour injures him
only too literally (see Act III Scene 1).
82 **contrary** defy
time that is, time to tell you off for your behaviour
83 **princox** impertinent youngster
86 **perforce** enforced
87 **different greeting** clash of opposites (that is,
patience and anger. It is ironic that Tybalt sees
himself as the patient one!)
89 **gall** poison

Tybalt Uncle, this is a Montague, our foe:
A villain that is hither come in spite
To scorn at our solemnity this night.   60

Capulet Young Romeo is it?

Tybalt   'Tis he, that villain Romeo.

Capulet Content thee, gentle coz, let him alone,
'A bears him like a portly gentleman;
And, to say truth, Verona brags of him
To be a virtuous and well-governed youth.   65
I would not for the wealth of all this town
Here in my house do him disparagement.
Therefore be patient, take no note of him.
It is my will, the which if thou respect,
Show a fair presence and put off these frowns,   70
An ill-beseeming semblance for a feast.

Tybalt It fits when such a villain is a guest:
I'll not endure him.

Capulet   He shall be endured.
What, goodman boy! I say he shall! Go to,
Am I the master here or you? Go to.   75
You'll not endure him! God shall mend my soul,
You'll make a mutiny among my guests,
You will set cock-a-hoop, you'll be the man!

Tybalt Why, uncle, 'tis a shame.

Capulet   Go to, go to.
You are a saucy boy. Is't so indeed?   80
This trick may chance to scathe you. I know what.
You must contrary me. Marry, 'tis time –
Well said, my hearts – You are a princox, go
Be quiet, or – More light! More light! – For shame,
I'll make you quiet. What, cheerly, my hearts!   85

Tybalt Patience perforce with wilful choler meeting
Makes my flesh tremble in their different greeting.
I will withdraw; but this intrusion shall
Now seeming sweet, convert to bitt'rest gall.   [*Exit*]

Romeo If I profane with my unworthiest hand   90

He kisses her

Victoria Theatre 1968

This holy shrine, the gentle sin is this:
My lips, two blushing pilgrims, ready stand
To smooth that rough touch with a tender kiss.

Juliet   Good pilgrim, you do wrong your hand too much,
Which mannerly devotion shows in this;   95
For saints have hands that pilgrims' hands do touch,
And palm to palm is holy palmers' kiss.

Romeo   Have not saints lips, and holy palmers too?

Juliet   Ay, pilgrim, lips that they must use in prayer.

Romeo   O then, dear saint, let lips do what hands do: 100
They pray 'Grant thou, lest faith turn to despair.'

Juliet   Saints do not move, though grant for prayer's sake.

Romeo   Then move not, while my prayer's effect I take.

[He kisses her]

Thus from my lips, by thine, my sin is purged.

Juliet   Then have my lips the sin that they have took.   105

Romeo   Sin from my lips? O trespass sweetly urged.
Give me my sin again.   *[He kisses her]*

Juliet   You kiss by th'book.

Nurse   Madam, your mother craves a word with you.

Romeo   What is her mother?

Nurse   Marry bachelor,
Her mother is the lady of the house,   110
And a good lady, and a wise and virtuous.
I nursed her daughter that you talked withal.
I tell you, he that can lay hold of her
Shall have the chinks.

Romeo   Is she a Capulet?
O dear account. My life is my foe's debt.   115

Benvolio   Away, be gone, the sport is at the best.

Romeo   Ay, so I fear; the more is my unrest.

Capulet   *[To the* **Maskers***]* Nay, gentlemen, prepare not to be
gone,

91   **This holy shrine**   that is, Juliet's hand (which, it must be presumed, he has taken in his own hand)
gentle sin   The meaning is unclear, but Romeo may be anticipating the kiss mentioned in the following two lines.
92   **pilgrims**   because they intend reverently to 'visit' Juliet's hand
95   **mannerly**   proper
96   **saints**   statues and images of saints
97   **palmers**   pilgrims who had been to Jerusalem At one time such pilgrims carried a palm leaf to show that they had been there. Can you explain how Juliet is punning on 'palm'?
101   **'Grant thou, lest faith turn to despair'**   that is, grant me a kiss lest my faith (in your love) turn to despair (a state of sin)
103   **my prayer's effect**   that is, a kiss
104   **purged**   cleaned away
106   **urged**   argued
107   **by th' book**   like an expert who has studied a book on the subject
108   Whereabouts on the stage do you suppose the Nurse has been during the exchange between Romeo and Juliet? In what way would you advise her to approach them? Has she seen or overheard them? Is she interrupting now to stop matters going further?
109   **What**   who
Presumably Juliet immediately rejoins her mother.
Marry bachelor   indeed (literally, by the Virgin Mary), young man
112   **withal**   with
114   **chinks**   plenty of money (because Juliet is Capulet's only heir)
115   **dear account**   costly reckoning
my foe's debt   owing to my enemy
116   See Act I Scene 4 line 39.
117   **unrest**   uneasiness
What is it that Romeo fears?
121–2   What part of Capulet's character do these lines emphasise?

Examine the language before and after Tybalt's exit, and show how it helps to create a change of mood in the dramatic situation.

Why do you think Romeo and Juliet indulge in religious imagery here?

Young Vic 1987–8

119 **trifling foolish banquet** light refreshments (of the dessert variety – usually sweets, fruit and wine)
towards just arriving
120 What excuses do you think the maskers whisper to Capulet that prompts him knowingly to say, 'Is it e'en so'?
121 **honest** honourable
123 **sirrah** See line 27 of this scene.
fay faith
waxes grows
125–7 Why does Juliet first ask about two other young men?
132 In what way will this line be seen to be grimly ironic in view of future events?
135 **only hate** To what is she referring?
136 I saw him before I knew who he was, and now I know it is too late (because I am irreversibly in love).
137 **Prodigious** monstrous and ill-omened
139 **What's this? What's this?** Why do you think the Nurse says this? Does she hear what Juliet has just said?
140 **Anon** at once

Look back at what Romeo says about love in Act I Scene 1. Compare this with his encounter with Juliet in Act I Scene 5.

Show how Shakespeare has set the theme as well as the scene of the play by the end of Act I.

Go ask his name.

Royal Shakespeare Company 1961

We have a trifling foolish banquet towards.

[*They whisper in his ear*]

Is it e'en so? Why then, I thank you all;   120
I thank you honest gentlemen, good night.
More torches here. Come on then, let's to bed.
Ah sirrah, by my fay, it waxes late,
I'll to my rest.

[*Exeunt* **Capulet, Lady Capulet, Guests, Gentlewomen**
and **Maskers**]

Juliet   Come hither Nurse. What is yond gentleman?   125

Nurse   The son and heir of old Tiberio.

Juliet   What's he that now is going out of door?

Nurse   Marry, that I think be young Petruchio.

Juliet   What's he that follows here, that would not dance?

Nurse   I know not.   130

Juliet   Go ask his name. If he be married,
My grave is like to be my wedding bed.

Nurse   His name is Romeo, and a Montague,
The only son of your great enemy.

Juliet   My only love sprung from my only hate.   135
Too early seen unknown, and known too late.
Prodigious birth of love it is to me
That I must love a loathed enemy.

Nurse   What's this? What's this?

Juliet   A rhyme I learned even now
Of one I danced withal.   [*One calls from offstage: 'Juliet'*]

Nurse   Anon, anon!   140
Come let's away, the strangers all are gone.

[*Exeunt*]

Act II

Enter **Chorus**.

Chorus   Now old desire doth in his deathbed lie
And young affection gapes to be his heir;
That fair for which love groaned for and would die,
With tender Juliet matched, is now not fair.
Now Romeo is beloved and loves again,   5
Alike bewitched by the charm of looks,
But to his foe supposed he must complain
And she steal love's sweet bait from fearful hooks.
Being held a foe, he may not have access
To breathe such vows as lovers use to swear;   10
And she as much in love, her means much less
To meet her new beloved anywhere.
But passion lends them power, time means, to meet,
Tempering extremities with extreme sweet.   [*Exit*]

Scene 1

A lane running by Capulet's orchard. Enter **Romeo** *alone.*

Romeo   Can I go forward when my heart is here?
Turn back, dull earth, and find thy centre out.
                                          [*Withdraws*]

1 **old desire**   that is, Romeo's old lust for Rosaline
2 **young affection**   Given the note to line 1, to what
do you think this refers?
gapes . . . heir   eagerly awaits, as if with open
mouth
3 **fair**   fair beauty (Rosaline)
love   that is, the lover (Romeo)
4 **matched**   compared
5 **again**   in return
6 **Alike**   each of them, both
7 **complain**   make his lament of love (or 'groan' for
love – see line 3)
Why might Juliet be supposed Romeo's 'foe'?
8 **fearful**   dangerous
The image is of a fish who tries to steal bait without
becoming hooked.
9 **held**   considered
10 **use**   are accustomed
11 **means**   opportunity
14 mitigating the extreme difficulties of their situation
with the great sweetness of their meetings
1 **forward**   that is, physically away
2 **dull earth**   that is, Romeo's body, which he thinks
of as heavy and uninspiring
centre   his heart, and so by implication Juliet, who
now possesses his heart and is the centre of his
world

What are the advantages and disadvantages
of using a Chorus? (You may like to have a
look at Shakespeare's use of the Chorus in
Henry V.)

**And she steal love's sweet bait from
fearful hooks.**

6 conjure conjure him up (as if he were a spirit)
7 Humours! moody! (like a lover)
11 gossip Venus my close friend Venus, goddess of love
fair pleasant
12 purblind totally blind
13 Abraham Cupid rogue Cupid (god of love) Abraham men were rogues who begged their way in Elizabethan times. It is also possible that 'Abraham' means as old as the patriach of the Old Testament; for Cupid, although a boy, was one of the oldest gods.
14 In an old ballad King Cophetua fell in love with a beggar girl (demonstrating Cupid's skill in shooting his arrows so **trim** that he creates unlikely matches).
15 He that is, Romeo
16 ape is dead like a performing ape in a fairground which pretends to be dead until raised by its master
18 A high forehead was considered beautiful.
20 demesnes areas
21 Mercutio still speaks as if Romeo has become a spirit.
23-6 'Twould anger . . . down The general sense of this is that Romeo would be angry if another man were spirited up as a lover of Rosaline. However, a sexual double-meaning runs through the lines.
26 until she had exorcised the spirit of the other man (that is, rejected him)
27 spite spitefulness, malice
invocation spell cast to summon up (Romeo)
28 fair and honest perfectly proper
29 raise that is, like a spirit (but with sexual double-meaning)
31 consorted associated with
humorous (i) damp; (ii) of melancholy mood
32 befits suits
33 mark target (with sexual double-meaning)
34,36 medlar The medlar fruit was a vulgar name for female private parts, and 'meddle' was slang for sexual activity.

What is your opinion of Mercutio as he presents himself here?

Although there is no break in the action, there is a change of mood between Scenes 1 and 2. Describe this change, and how it is created. Pay attention to the language.

[*Enter* **Benvolio** *with* **Mercutio**]

Benvolio   Romeo! My cousin Romeo! Romeo!
Mercutio   He is wise,
And on my life hath stol'n him home to bed.
Benvolio   He ran this way and leapt this orchard wall.   5
Call, good Mercutio.
Mercutio   Nay, I'll conjure too:
Romeo! Humours! Madman! Passion! Lover!
Appear thou in the likeness of a sigh,
Speak but one rhyme and I am satisfied.
Cry but 'Ay me!' Pronounce but 'love' and 'dove',   10
Speak to my gossip Venus one fair word,
One nickname for her purblind son and heir,
Young Abraham Cupid, he that shot so trim
When King Cophetua loved the beggar maid.
He heareth not, he stirreth not, he moveth not: 15
The ape is dead and I must conjure him.
I conjure thee by Rosaline's bright eyes,
By her high forehead and her scarlet lip,
By her fine foot, straight leg, and quivering thigh,
And the demesnes that there adjacent lie,   20
That in thy likeness thou appear to us.
Benvolio   And if he hear thee, thou wilt anger him.
Mercutio   This cannot anger him. 'Twould anger him
To raise a spirit in his mistress' circle
Of some strange nature, letting it there stand   25
Till she had laid it and conjured it down:
That were some spite. My invocation
Is fair and honest; in his mistress' name
I conjure only but to raise up him.
Benvolio   Come, he hath hid himself among these trees   30
To be consorted with the humorous night.
Blind is his love, and best befits the dark.
Mercutio   If love be blind, love cannot hit the mark.
Now will he sit under a medlar tree
And wish his mistress were that kind of fruit   35

If love be blind, love cannot hit the mark.

As maids call medlars when they laugh alone.
O Romeo, that she were, O that she were
An open-arse and thou a poperin pear!
Romeo, good night. I'll to my truckle-bed.
This field-bed is too cold for me to sleep.   40
Come, shall we go?

Benvolio   Go then, for 'tis in vain
To seek him here that means not to be found.

[*Exeunt* **Benvolio** *and* **Mercutio**]

Scene 2

Capulet's orchard. **Romeo** *comes forward.*

Romeo   He jests at scars that never felt a wound.

[*Enter* **Juliet** *above*]

But soft, what light through yonder window breaks?
It is the east and Juliet is the sun!
Arise fair sun and kill the envious moon
Who is already sick and pale with grief   5
That thou her maid art far more fair than she.
Be not her maid since she is envious,
Her vestal livery is but sick and green
And none but fools do wear it. Cast it off.
It is my lady, O it is my love!   10
O that she knew she were!
She speaks, yet she says nothing. What of that?
Her eye discourses, I will answer it.
I am too bold. 'Tis not to me she speaks.
Two of the fairest stars in all the heaven,   15
Having some business, do entreat her eyes
To twinkle in their spheres till they return.
What if her eyes were there, they in her head?

38 **open-arse** country name for the medlar
poperin type of pear from Flanders which, because of its shape, was a vulgar name for 'penis'
39 **truckle-bed** small (cosy) bed
40 **field-bed** camp bed
sleep sleep on

1 **He** that is, Mercutio
scars scoffs
wound that is, of love
This is ironic in view of the fatal physical wound which Mercutio is later to suffer.
2 **soft** hush! just a minute!
3 Why do you think Romeo sees Juliet as the sun?
6 Diana was the Roman goddess of the moon and of chastity, and Romeo is saying that she is envious because Juliet, a handmaid of Diana because a virgin, is fairer than she.
8 **vestal** virgin
sick and green refers to (i) the paleness of the moon; (ii) the fact that young girls of marriageable age were supposed to be susceptible to 'green-sickness', a kind of anaemia
9 **fools** Green would have been one of the colours worn by jesters as part of their suit of motley colours.
12 **She ... nothing** Presumably Romeo can see her lips move, but cannot hear what she says.
13 **discourses** speaks (that is, tells much about what is in her mind)
15 **stars** planets
16 **business** that is, affairs which take them away from home

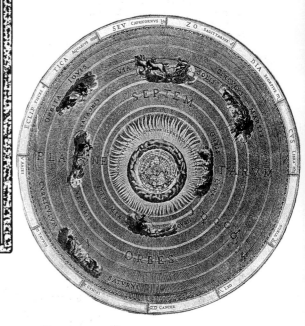

17 **spheres** orbits
According to the ancient theories of Ptolemy, the stars and planets were fixed upon crystal spheres which enclosed the earth in layers. See the illustration above.
18 **there** that is, in place of the absent spheres
they that is, the spheres

It is my lady ...

Albany Empire 1988

21 airy region sky or heavens
        What image do you think Shakespeare is trying to
        summon up by using the verb **stream**?
28 winged messenger angel
29 Explain the image in this line.
30 fall back lean backwards
33 wherefore why
34 refuse reject, renounce
35 be but sworn simply swear that you are
39 though even if you were
46 owes owns
47 doff throw off (as one might a coat or hat)
48 for as payment for
50 Call me but only call me

Ay me!

Albany Empire 1988

> The brightness of her cheek would shame those stars
> As daylight doth a lamp. Her eyes in heaven   20
> Would through the airy region stream so bright
> That birds would sing and think it were not night.
> See how she leans her cheek upon her hand.
> O that I were a glove upon that hand,
> That I might touch that cheek!

Juliet   Ay me!

Romeo   She speaks.   25
> O speak again bright angel, for thou art
> As glorious to this night, being o'er my head,
> As is a winged messenger of heaven
> Unto the white-upturned wondering eyes
> Of mortals that fall back to gaze on him   30
> When he bestrides the lazy-puffing clouds
> And sails upon the bosom of the air.

Juliet   O Romeo, Romeo, wherefore art thou Romeo?
> Deny thy father and refuse thy name.
> Or if thou wilt not, be but sworn my love   35
> And I'll no longer be a Capulet.

Romeo   Shall I hear more, or shall I speak at this?

Juliet   'Tis but thy name that is my enemy:
> Thou art thyself, though not a Montague.
> What's Montague? It is nor hand nor foot   40
> Nor arm nor face nor any other part
> Belonging to a man. O be some other name.
> What's in a name? That which we call a rose
> By any other word would smell as sweet;
> So Romeo would, were he not Romeo called,   45
> Retain that dear perfection which he owes
> Without that title. Romeo, doff thy name,
> And for thy name, which is no part of thee,
> Take all myself.

Romeo   I take thee at thy word.
> Call me but love, and I'll be new baptised: 50
> Henceforth I never will be Romeo.

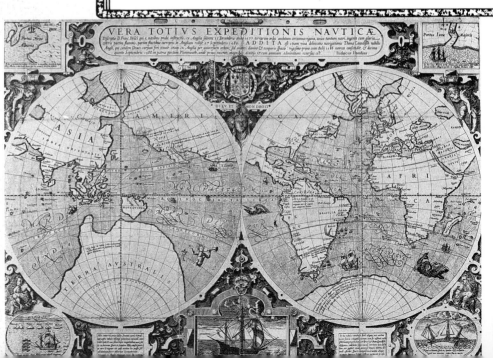

Map of Elizabethan world,
showing routes of voyages
of discovery. See lines 82-4
opposite.

Juliet What man art thou that thus bescreened in night
So stumblest on my counsel?

Romeo   By a name
I know not how to tell thee who I am:
My name, dear saint, is hateful to myself   55
Because it is an enemy to thee.
Had I it written, I would tear the word.

Juliet My ears have yet not drunk a hundred words
Of thy tongue's uttering, yet I know the sound.
Art thou not Romeo, and a Montague?   60

Romeo Neither, fair maid, if either thee dislike.

Juliet How cam'st thou hither, tell me, and wherefore?
The orchard walls are high and hard to climb,
And the place death, considering who thou art,
If any of my kinsmen find thee here.   65

Romeo With love's light wings did I o'erperch these walls,
For stony limits cannot hold love out,
And what love can do, that dares love attempt:
Therefore thy kinsmen are no stop to me.

Juliet If they do see thee, they will murder thee.   70

Romeo Alack, there lies more peril in thine eye
Than twenty of their swords. Look thou but sweet
And I am proof against their enmity.

Juliet I would not for the world they saw thee here.

Romeo I have night's cloak to hide me from their eyes, 75
And but thou love me, let them find me here.
My life were better ended by their hate
Than death prorogued, wanting of thy love.

Juliet By whose direction found'st thou out this place?

Romeo By love, that first did prompt me to enquire.   80
He lent me counsel, and I lent him eyes.
I am no pilot, yet wert thou as far
As that vast shore washed with the farthest sea,
I should adventure for such merchandise.

Juliet Thou knowest the mask of night is on my face,   85

---

52 **bescreened** hidden as if behind a screen
53 **counsel** private thoughts (spoken aloud, according to the convention of soliloquy on the Elizabethan stage)
55 Why does Romeo call her 'dear saint'? What is he echoing?
66 **o'erperch** fly over
67 **stony limits** boundaries made of stone
68 **that . . . attempt** love will dare to attempt it
71-2 **Alack . . . swords** What do you think Romeo means by this? In what way do these words become ironic?
72 **Look thou but sweet** just look at me nicely
73 **proof** protected
76 **but** unless
78 **prorogued** delayed, postponed
   wanting of lacking
82 **pilot** navigator
   There is recurring imagery in the play of Romeo as an adventurer on the seas who is, unknown to himself, steering a tragic course. See Act I Scene 4 line 112 and Act V Scene 3 lines 117-18.
83 **vast** (i) large; (ii) waste, barren
   Find out why nautical imagery may have been particularly appropriate to the age in which this play was written.
   farthest sea that is, the outer limits of current exploration
84 **adventure** The word is often used in connection with merchant adventurers.

> What aspects of Juliet's character reveal themselves here?

> Draw a stage plan showing how you would design this scene. Where would Romeo hide? Would you put Juliet up on the traditional balcony?

Theatre Royal, Covent Garden 1753

88 Fain gladly
    dwell on form observe formal behaviour (it was
    quite inappropriate for a lady to be too easily won)
89 compliment conventional, formal speech and
    manners
92 perjuries lies, broken oaths
96 say thee nay refuse you
97 So thou wilt woo provided that you continue to
    woo me
    else otherwise
98 fond helplessly in love
99 haviour behaviour
101, strange reserved, coldly distant
102 Juliet is referring to ladies who cleverly seem hard
    to win in order to keep their lovers at their feet.
102 should have been intended to be
103 ere before
    ware aware (of your presence)
105 not do not
    light See line 99.
106 Which referring to **yielding**
    dark Note the play on words with **light** in the
    previous line.
107–8 What kind of typical language is Romeo beginning
    to talk before he is interrupted by Juliet?
109– th' inconstant . . . changes The moon was often
10 taken as a symbol of inconstancy. Why?
110 circled orb the crystal sphere upon which the
    moon moved in orbit, according to the old
    Ptolemaic astronomy (see note to line 17)
115 What do you think Romeo is about to say?
117 contract exchange of lovers' vows
118 unadvised decided without proper thought

Re-read lines 1–154 of this scene and
consider (a) presentation of characters,
(b) dramatic interest, and (c) poetic qualities.

Do not swear at all.

Royal Theatre Northampton 1982

Else would a maiden blush bepaint my cheek
For that which thou hast heard me speak tonight.
Fain would I dwell on form; fain, fain deny
What I have spoke. But farewell, compliment.
Dost thou love me? I know thou wilt say 'Ay',   90
And I will take thy word. Yet, if thou swear'st,
Thou mayst prove false. At lovers' perjuries,
They say, Jove laughs. O gentle Romeo,
If thou dost love, pronounce it faithfully.
Or, if thou think'st I am too quickly won,   95
I'll frown and be perverse and say thee nay,
So thou wilt woo; but else, not for the world.
In truth, fair Montague, I am too fond,
And therefore thou mayst think my haviour light,
But trust me, gentleman, I'll prove more true   100
Than those that have more cunning to be strange.
I should have been more strange, I must confess,
But that thou overheard'st, ere I was ware,
My true-love passion; therefore pardon me,
And not impute this yielding to light love   105
Which the dark night hath so discovered.

Romeo   Lady, by yonder blessed moon I vow,
That tips with silver all these fruit-tree tops –

Juliet   O swear not by the moon, th'inconstant moon,
That monthly changes in her circled orb,   110
Lest that thy love prove likewise variable.

Romeo   What shall I swear by?

Juliet   Do not swear at all.
Or if thou wilt, swear by thy gracious self,
Which is the god of my idolatry,
And I'll believe thee.

Romeo   If my heart's dear love –   115

Juliet   Well, do not swear. Although I joy in thee,
I have no joy of this contract tonight:
It is too rash, too unadvised, too sudden,
Too like the lightning, which doth cease to be

Ere one can say 'It lightens'. Sweet, good night. 120
This bud of love, by summer's ripening breath,
May prove a beauteous flower when next we meet.
Good night, good night. As sweet repose and rest
Come to thy heart as that within my breast.

Romeo   O wilt thou leave me so unsatisfied? 125

Juliet   What satisfaction canst thou have tonight?

Romeo   Th'exchange of thy love's faithful vow for mine.

Juliet   I gave thee mine before thou didst request it,
And yet I would it were to give again.

Romeo   Wouldst thou withdraw it? For what purpose, love? 130

Juliet   But to be frank and give it thee again;
And yet I wish but for the thing I have.
My bounty is as boundless as the sea,
My love as deep: the more I give to thee
The more I have, for both are infinite. 135
I hear some noise within. Dear love, adieu.

                          [**Nurse** *calls within*]
Anon, good Nurse – Sweet Montague be true.
Stay but a little, I will come again.   [*Exit* **Juliet**]

Romeo   O blessed blessed night. I am afeard,
Being in night, all this is but a dream, 140
Too flattering sweet to be substantial.

[*Enter* **Juliet** *above*]

Juliet   Three words, dear Romeo, and good night indeed.
If that thy bent of love be honourable,
Thy purpose marriage, send me word tomorrow
By one that I'll procure to come to thee, 145
Where and what time thou wilt perform the rite,
And all my fortunes at thy foot I'll lay,
And follow thee my lord throughout the world.

Nurse   [*Within*] Madam.

Juliet   I come, anon – But if thou meanest not well 150
I do beseech thee –

124 **that**   to that heart which is
131 **But**   simply
    frank   generous, freely spoken
132 **but**   only
133 **bounty**   generosity
133–4 Note that here is more sea imagery.
137 **Anon**   (coming) immediately
141 **flattering**   deceitfully (because flattery is often insincere)
    substantial   (pronounced with four syllables)   real
143 **bent**   tendency, inclination
145 **procure**   arrange, fix
146 **rite**   To what rite is she referring?
150 What does she mean by **But if . . . well**?

Stay but a little, I will come again.

Bristol Old Vic 1966

151 By and by immediately
152 strife attempt (to woo me)
153 So thrive my soul as I hope that God will save my soul
Juliet interrupts Romeo. What do you think he was about to say?

155 want thy light lack the illumination of your presence (because night is black)
Look back at lines 1–32 of this scene, and make a list of all the images of light which Romeo uses in those lines. Why do you think they recur, and what effect do they give?

159 tassel-gentle male hawk (**gentle** means literally 'gentleman' or 'noble')
160 Bondage is hoarse Juliet means that she must whisper because she is confined within the discipline of her father's house.
161 tear that is, with sound
Echo In classical mythology Echo, her love rejected by Narcissus, lived in a cave and was wasted away by grief until only her voice was left.
162 airy tongue Echo has no physical tongue.
164 Why do you think Romeo calls Juliet **my soul**?
165 silver-sweet See Act IV Scene 5 lines 126–35.
166 nyas a young hawk still in its nest (and which, therefore, has never flown)
169 Does Juliet fail? See Act II Scene 4, and find out what time the Nurse actually meets Romeo on the following day.
172 still (i) forever, (ii) without moving
173 Remembering while I think about
Shakespeare amuses the audience by re-creating the age-old scene of lovers who cannot finally say goodbye to each other.
177 wanton spoilt child

Nurse [*Within*]   Madam.

Juliet   By and by I come –
To cease thy strife and leave me to my grief.
Tomorrow will I send.

Romeo   So thrive my soul –

Juliet A thousand times good night.   [*Exit* **Juliet**]

Romeo A thousand times the worse, to want thy light.   155
Love goes toward love as schoolboys from their books,
But love from love, toward school with heavy looks.

[*Enter* **Juliet** *above again*]

Juliet Hist! Romeo, hist! O for a falconer's voice
To lure this tassel-gentle back again.
Bondage is hoarse and may not speak aloud,   160
Else would I tear the cave where Echo lies
And make her airy tongue more hoarse than mine
With repetition of my Romeo's name.

Romeo It is my soul that calls upon my name.
How silver-sweet sound lovers' tongues by night,   165
Like softest music to attending ears.

Juliet Romeo.

Romeo   My nyas.

Juliet   What o'clock tomorrow
Shall I send to thee?

Romeo   By the hour of nine.

Juliet I will not fail. 'Tis twenty year till then.
I have forgot why I did call thee back.   170

Romeo Let me stand here till thou remember it.

Juliet I shall forget, to have thee still stand there,
Remembering how I love thy company.

Romeo And I'll still stay to have thee still forget,
Forgetting any other home but this.   175

Juliet 'Tis almost morning, I would have thee gone,
And yet no farther than a wanton's bird,

Good night, good night!

Orchard Theatre 1986

Parting is such sweet sorrow

Redgrave Theatre 1974

That lets it hop a little from his hand
Like a poor prisoner in his twisted gyves,
And with a silken thread plucks it back again,
So loving-jealous of his liberty.   180

Romeo   I would I were thy bird.

Juliet   Sweet, so would I:
Yet I should kill thee with much cherishing.
Good night, good night! Parting is such sweet sorrow
That I shall say good night till it be morrow.   185

                                        [*Exit* **Juliet**]

Romeo   Sleep dwell upon thine eyes, peace in thy breast.
Would I were sleep and peace so sweet to rest.
The grey-eyed morn smiles on the frowning night,
Chequering the eastern clouds with streaks of light;
And darkness fleckled like a drunkard reels   190
From forth day's pathway, made by Titan's wheels.
Hence will I to my ghostly Sire's close cell,
His help to crave and my dear hap to tell.

                                                        [*Exit*]

Scene 3

Verona. **Friar Laurence's** *cell. Enter* **Friar Laurence** *alone with
a basket.*

Friar Laurence   Now, ere the sun advance his burning eye
The day to cheer, and night's dank dew to dry,
I must upfill this osier cage of ours
With baleful weeds and precious-juiced flowers.
The earth that's nature's mother is her tomb: 5
What is her burying grave, that is her womb;
And from her womb children of divers kind
We sucking on her natural bosom find.
Many for many virtues excellent,
None but for some, and yet all different.   10
O, mickle is the powerful grace that lies
In plants, herbs, stones, and their true qualities.

179 **gyves**   fetters, shackles (The child ties a **silken thread** to the bird's leg, lets it hop away a little, and then hauls it back again.)
181 **loving-jealous of his liberty**   that is, the child loves the bird and so jealously prevents it from gaining its liberty
183   an ominous line
187   I wish that I were the personification of sleep and peace so that I could rest in such a sweet place (as Juliet's eyes and breast)
188 **grey-eyed**   It is probable that Elizabethans referred to blue eyes as 'grey'. See Act II Scene 4 line 39 and note.
190 **fleckled**   dappled with light
191 **From forth**   out of the way of
Titan's wheels   that is, the sun
According to classical legend, Hyperion, the sun god, was a Titan, who rode across the sky every day in his burning chariot.
192   From here I will go to my spiritual father's secluded cell
193 **dear hap**   good fortune

1 **advance**   raise up
3 **osier cage**   willow basket
ours   belonging to the Franciscan order, of which Friar Laurence is a member
4 **baleful**   poisonous, full of evil
precious-juiced   because they contain healing properties
5   that is, all living things come from the earth and return to it
7 **divers**   various
8 **sucking**   sustenance
9 **virtues**   health-giving or healing properties
10 **None but for some**   all are good for something
11 **mickle**   great
grace   divine effectiveness

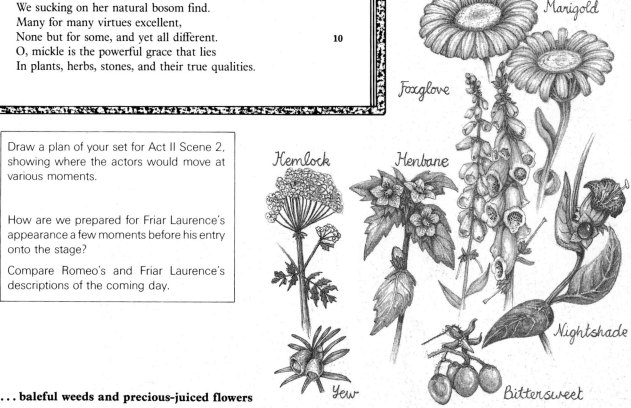

Draw a plan of your set for Act II Scene 2, showing where the actors would move at various moments.

How are we prepared for Friar Laurence's appearance a few moments before his entry onto the stage?

Compare Romeo's and Friar Laurence's descriptions of the coming day.

... baleful weeds and precious-juiced flowers

13 **For naught so vile** for there is nothing so worthless
earth inhabitants of the earth
15 **aught** anything
strained . . . use perverted from its proper use
16 turns from its proper nature, when abused
18 and faults, in certain circumstances, result in good
19 **infant rind** fresh skin
20 both poison and healing powers dwell
21 **with that part** that is, its smell
22 **stays . . . heart** stops the heart, and thus all the body's senses
23 **still** always
24 **grace** attributes which lead to divine mercy
rude will fleshly (earth-bound) desires
25 Which is **the worser**?
26 **Full** very
canker caterpillar
27 **Benedicite** (Latin) Bless you!
28 **early tongue** Is Romeo's **tongue** literally **early**? What does Friar Laurence mean? (This device is known as a 'transferred epithet'.)
29 **argues** demonstrates, shows
distempered head disturbed mind
30 **good morrow** goodbye
31 In what way do you think **Care keeps his watch**?
33 **unbruised** undamaged (by life's experience)
unstuffed not full (of troubles)
36 **distemperature** See line 29.
40-1 Why are we reminded of Rosaline at this point?
41 **ghostly** spiritual

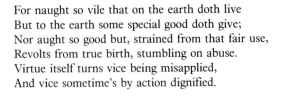

For naught so vile that on the earth doth live
But to the earth some special good doth give;
Nor aught so good but, strained from that fair use,   15
Revolts from true birth, stumbling on abuse.
Virtue itself turns vice being misapplied,
And vice sometime's by action dignified.

[*Enter* **Romeo**]

Within the infant rind of this weak flower
Poison hath residence, and medicine power: 20
For this, being smelt, with that part cheers each part;
Being tasted, stays all senses with the heart.
Two such opposed kings encamp them still
In man as well as herbs: grace and rude will;
And where the worser is predominant   25
Full soon the canker death eats up that plant.

Romeo   Good morrow, father.

Friar Laurence   Benedicite.
What early tongue so sweet saluteth me?
Young son, it argues a distempered head
So soon to bid good morrow to thy bed.   30
Care keeps his watch in every old man's eye,
And where care lodges sleep will never lie,
But where unbruised youth with unstuffed brain
Doth couch his limbs, there golden sleep doth reign.
Therefore thy earliness doth me assure   35
Thou art uproused with some distemperature;
Or, if not so, then here I hit it right:
Our Romeo hath not been in bed tonight.

Romeo   That last is true. The sweeter rest was mine.

Father Laurence   God pardon sin. Wast thou with Rosaline?   40

Romeo   With Rosaline! My ghostly father, no.
I have forgot that name, and that name's woe.

Father Laurence   That's my good son. But where hast thou been then?

How does Friar Laurence's opening soliloquy, and what he says in this scene as a whole, prepare us for his character and actions later in the play?

In the light of later events, what is ironic about Friar Laurence's thoughts at the moment of Romeo's entry?

Zeffirelli 1968

Choose words from the text on this page which you think would provide the best caption for this picture.

Romeo   I'll tell thee ere thou ask it me again.
I have been feasting with mine enemy,   45
Where on a sudden one hath wounded me
That's by me wounded. Both our remedies
Within thy help and holy physic lies.
I bear no hatred, blessed man, for lo,
My intercession likewise steads my foe.   50

Friar Laurence   Be plain, good son, and homely in thy drift;
Riddling confession finds but riddling shrift.

Romeo   Then plainly know my heart's dear love is set
On the fair daughter of rich Capulet.
As mine on hers, so hers is set on mine,   55
And all combined save what thou must combine
By holy marriage. When, and where, and how
We met, we wooed, and made exchange of vow
I'll tell thee as we pass; but this I pray,
That thou consent to marry us today.   60

Friar Laurence   Holy Saint Francis! What a change is here!
Is Rosaline, that thou didst love so dear,
So soon forsaken? Young men's love then lies
Not truly in their hearts but in their eyes.
Jesu Maria! What a deal of brine   65
Hath washed thy sallow cheeks for Rosaline.
How much salt water thrown away in waste
To season love, that of it doth not taste.
The sun not yet thy sighs from heaven clears,
Thy old groans yet ring in mine ancient ears.   70
Lo here upon thy cheek the stain doth sit
Of an old tear that is not washed off yet.
If e'er thou wast thyself, and these woes thine,
Thou and these woes were all for Rosaline.
And art thou changed? Pronounce this sentence then: 75
Women may fall when there's no strength in men.

Romeo   Thou chid'st me oft for loving Rosaline.

Friar Laurence   For doting, not for loving, pupil mine.

Romeo   And bad'st me bury love.

46–7   **Where . . . by me wounded** a reference to Cupid's arrows
Who was Cupid? Who is the **enemy** in line 45, **one** in line 46, and to whom does **That's** refer in line 47?
48   **physic** medicine
What kind of **physic** has Romeo in mind?
49   **hatred** that is, towards my foe (Juliet)
lo look, see
50   **intercession** holy petition
steads benefits
51   **homely** straightforward
drift meaning
52   **Riddling** unclear, ambiguous
Friar Laurence means that if a confession is not straightforward, then a priest cannot offer proper absolution (**shrift**).
54   What evidence have we had that Capulet is a **rich** man?
56   **all combined** both of us are of one mind
59   **pass** go along
Is it typical of Romeo to be in a hurry?
61   **Francis** It is acceptable for Friar Laurence to swear by the patron saint of his order (Franciscan).
63–4   **Young men's . . . eyes** What do these lines mean? Can you find other places in the play where judgement is made through the eyes? Is this a safe way to judge?
65   **Jesu Maria** by Jesus and Mary (another mild oath suitable to a priest)
brine salt tears
68   **season** Salt is a preservative and adds flavour to food.
it love
69   The idea is of the sun melting away the vapour made by the sighs of a lover.
73   **e'er** ever
wast thyself that is, sincere
75   **sentence** proverb
76   **fall** be excused for unfaithfulness
strength fidelity
77   **chid'st me oft** often told me off
78   **pupil mine** How does Friar Laurence regard Romeo? What tone of voice should be adopted by the actor playing the Friar?

Compass Theatre Company
1987–8

80 **one** one love
82 **grace** favour
allow return; that is, Juliet returns his love (unlike Rosaline)
83–4 Rosaline well understood that Romeo's words of love were as if learnt by heart by one who could not actually read and understand (that is, he is not sincere).
86 **In one respect** for one reason
88 **To** so as to
In the light of the ending of the play, in what way could Friar Laurence's plan be seen as ironically successful?
89 **stand** insist

1 **should** can
2 **tonight** last night
3 **man** servant
7 **his** Romeo's
8 **on** I'll bet
9 **answer** accept the challenge
11 **master** that is, Tybalt
how showing how
15 **pin** dead centre of a target
blind bow-boy Cupid, god of love
16 **butt-shaft** an unbarbed arrow, used for archery practice in the butts

> Why do you think Shakespeare changes from verse to prose for Scene 4?

Temba Theatre Company 1988

Friar Laurence   Not in a grave
To lay one in, another out to have.   80

Romeo   I pray thee chide me not, her I love now
Doth grace for grace and love for love allow.
The other did not so.

Friar Laurence   O, she knew well
Thy love did read by rote that could not spell.
But come young waverer, come, go with me,   85
In one respect I'll thy assistant be.
For this alliance may so happy prove
To turn your households' rancour to pure love.

Romeo   O let us hence: I stand on sudden haste.

Friar Laurence   Wisely and slow; they stumble that run fast.   90

                    [*Exeunt*]

Scene 4

Verona. A street. Enter **Benvolio** *and* **Mercutio**.

Mercutio   Where the devil should this Romeo be? Came he not home tonight?

Benvolio   Not to his father's; I spoke with his man.

Mercutio   Why, that same pale hard-hearted wench, that Rosaline, torments him so that he will sure run mad.   5

Benvolio   Tybalt, the kinsman to old Capulet, hath sent a letter to his father's house.

Mercutio   A challenge, on my life.

Benvolio   Romeo will answer it.

Mercutio   Any man that can write may answer a letter.   10

Benvolio   Nay, he will answer the letter's master, how he dares, being dared.

Mercutio   Alas poor Romeo, he is already dead, stabbed with a white wench's black eye, run through the ear with a love song, the very pin of his heart cleft with the blind bow-boy's   15 butt-shaft. And is he a man to encounter Tybalt?

Benvolio   Why, what is Tybalt?

Mercutio   More than Prince of Cats. O, he's the courageous
captain of compliments: he fights as you sing prick-song,
keeps time, distance and proportion. He rests his minim rests, 20
one, two, and the third in your bosom: the very butcher of a
silk button – a duellist, a duellist, a gentleman of the very
first house, of the first and second cause. Ah, the immortal
passado, the punto reverso, the hay!

Benvolio   The what?   25

Mercutio   The pox of such antic lisping affecting fantasticoes,
these new tuners of accent. By Jesu, a very good blade, a very
tall man, a very good whore! Why, is not this a lamentable
thing, grandsire, that we should be thus afflicted with these
strange flies, these fashion-mongers, these 'pardon-me's', who 30
stand so much on the new form that they cannot sit at ease
on the old bench? O their bones, their bones!

[*Enter* **Romeo**]

Benvolio   Here comes Romeo, here comes Romeo!

Mercutio   Without his roe, like a dried herring. O flesh, flesh,
how art thou fishified. Now is he for the numbers that   35
Petrarch flowed in. Laura, to his lady, was a kitchen wench –
marry, she had a better love to berhyme her – Dido a dowdy,
Cleopatra a gypsy, Helen and Hero hildings and harlots,
Thisbe a grey eye or so, but not to the purpose. Signor
Romeo, bonjour. There's a French salutation to your French   40
slop. You gave us the counterfeit fairly last night.

Romeo   Good morrow to you both. What counterfeit did I
give you?

Mercutio   The slip sir, the slip. Can you not conceive?

Romeo   Pardon, good Mercutio, my business was great, and in 45
such a case as mine a man may strain courtesy.

Mercutio   That's as much as to say, such a case as yours
constrains a man to bow in the hams.

Romeo   Meaning to curtsy.

18 **Prince of Cats**   Tybalt was a cat in a popular
story.
19 **captain of compliments**   master of the
formalities of dwelling
During this speech Mercutio is making fun of the
elaborate set of rules of Italian fencing.
prick-song   printed music
20 **proportion**   rhythm
(Here, as in most places in this speech, the terms
can be applied to duelling or to music.)
minim rests   briefest of pauses in music
21-2 **butcher . . . button**   a skilful duellist could hit any
button on an opponent
23 **first house**   (i) best school; (ii) most important
family
first and second cause   stages in the
development of a quarrel
immortal   (i) famous; (ii) fatal
24 **passado**   lunging thrust
punto reverso   back-handed thrust
hay   hit
26 a plague on such grotesque lisping affected fops
27 **new . . . accent**   who speak in the latest
fashionable language
blade   swordsman
28 **tall**   valiant
29 **grandsire**   Mercutio pretends that he and Benvolio
are old men deploring the new ways of youth.
30 **strange flies**   alien parasites
'pardon-me's'   gallants who affect all the
courtesies
31 **stand**   insist (with a pun on the literal sense of the
word)
form   fashion in manners (with a pun on 'bench')
32 **the old bench . . . bones**   Enormous breeches
had gone out of fashion, and the new, thinner style
made the wooden seats seem hard.
34 **roe**   (i) only half himself; (ii) without his love
(Rosaline, thinks Mercutio), because a 'roe' was a
small deer
35 **fishified**   made cold-blooded (like a fish)
35-6 **for the numbers . . . flowed in**   inclined to
indulge in the kind of love poetry which Petrarch
wrote to Laura
to his   compared to Romeo's
37 **a better love**   that is, Petrarch
berhyme   make rhymes to
37-9 All the women mentioned here were famous as
loved ones.
38 **hildings**   good-for-nothings
39 **grey eye**   considered attractive by Elizabethans
not to the purpose   of no importance,
insignificant
40 **salutation to**   greeting suitable for
41 **slop**   breeches
Romeo is still wearing his masking costume from
the night before.
counterfeit   slip (a word for a counterfeit coin)
44 **conceive**   understand
46 **strain**   stretch, fall short in
48 **hams**   thighs (or, generally speaking, legs)

Temba Theatre Company 1988

> Discuss whatever you find interesting in the
> style, tone, subject-matter or language of
> Mercutio here. Is it typical of him?

50 **kindly hit**   accurately understood
51 **exposition**   explanation
52 **very pink**   highest degree (a **pink** is also a flower)
55 **pump**   light dancing shoe
    flowered   pricked with small holes for ornamentation (also known as 'pinked')
56 **Sure wit!**   clever chap!
57 **single**   thin
58 **solely singular**   by itself
59 **single-soled**   thin
    solely singular   unique
    singleness   silliness
60 Mercutio appeals to Benvolio as a referee. This duel of wits anticipates the more deadly duel to come later.
61 **Switch and spurs**   urge on your wit (as one might a horse)
61–2 **cry a match**   claim the victory
63 **wild-goose chase**   a cross-country race where everyone chased the leader; the pointlessness of it became proverbial
    done   exhausted
66 **goose**   (i) supposed to be a stupid bird; (ii) prostitute
    Mercutio's remark is difficult to interpret, but he seems to be saying, 'Did I keep up with your foolish jesting?' Romeo probably picks up the second meaning in line 68.
69 Biting the ear is a sign of affection, but Mercutio is mocking here.
71 **bitter sweeting**   a kind of apple, served with goose
    What comment do you think Mercutio is making on the nature of Romeo's wit?
74 **cheveril**   kid leather, which is easily stretched
75 **ell**   measure of 45 inches or 110 centimetres
76,77 **broad**   (i) obvious; (ii) rude
78 **this**   that is, this jesting
80 **art**   (second occurrence) skill
    nature   natural ability
81 **natural**   idiot
    lolling   with tongue hanging out
82 **bauble**   a professional jester's decorated stick (with an obscene secondary meaning)

Who do you think gets the better of the duel of wits, Romeo or Mercutio? Write notes for the actors indicating how they might perform this exchange. Should it be cut for a modern audience?

Mercutio   Thou hast most kindly hit it.   50

Romeo   A most courteous exposition.

Mercutio   Nay, I am the very pink of courtesy.

Romeo   Pink for flower.

Mercutio   Right.

Romeo   Why, then is my pump well flowered.   55

Mercutio   Sure wit! Follow me this jest now, till thou hast worn out thy pump, that when the single sole of it is worn, the jest may remain after the wearing solely singular.

Romeo   O single-soled jest, solely singular for the singleness.

Mercutio   Come between us, good Benvolio, my wits faints.   60

Romeo   Switch and spurs, switch and spurs, or I'll cry a match!

Mercutio   Nay, if our wits run the wild-goose chase I am done. For thou hast more of the wild-goose in one of thy wits than I am sure I have in my whole five. Was I with you there for the goose?   65

Romeo   Thou wast never with me for anything, when thou wast not there for the goose.

Mercutio   I will bite thee by the ear for that jest.

Romeo   Nay, good goose, bite not.   70

Mercutio   Thy wit is a very bitter sweeting, it is a most sharp sauce.

Romeo   And is it not then well served in to a sweet goose?

Mercutio   O here's a wit of cheveril, that stretches from an inch narrow to an ell broad.   75

Romeo   I stretch it out for that word 'broad', which, added to the goose, proves thee far and wide a broad goose.

Mercutio   Why, is not this better now than groaning for love? Now art thou sociable, now art thou Romeo; now art thou what thou art, by art as well as by nature. For this drivelling   80 love is like a great natural that runs lolling up and down to hide his bauble in a hole.

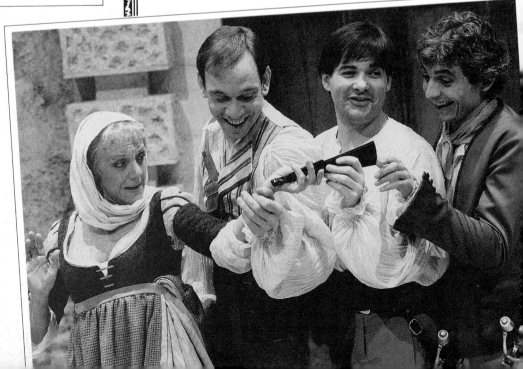

...to hide her face...

Bristol Old Vic 1983

Benvolio   Stop there, stop there.

Mercutio   Thou desirest me to stop in my tale against the hair.

Benvolio   Thou wouldst else have made thy tale large.   85

Mercutio   O, thou art deceived; I would have made it short; for I was come to the whole depth of my tale and meant indeed to occupy the argument no longer.

Romeo   Here's goodly gear.

[*Enter* **Nurse** *and* **Peter**, *her servant*]

A sail! A sail!   90

Mercutio   Two. Two. A shirt and a smock.

Nurse   Peter.

Peter   Anon.

Nurse   My fan, Peter.

Mercutio   Good Peter, to hide her face, for her fan's the fairer face.   95

Nurse   God ye good morrow, gentlemen.

Mercutio   God ye good e'en, fair gentlewoman.

Nurse   It is good e'en?

Mercutio   'Tis no less, I tell ye; for the bawdy hand of the dial is now upon the prick of noon.   100

Nurse   Out upon you. What a man are you?

Romeo   One, gentlewoman, that God hath made, himself to mar.

Nurse   By my troth it is well said; 'for himself to mar' quoth'a? Gentlemen, can any of you tell me where I may find the young Romeo?   105

Romeo   I can tell you; but young Romeo will be older when you have found him than he was when you sought him. I am the youngest of that name, for fault of a worse.   110

Nurse   You say well.

Mercutio   Yea, is the worst well? Very well took i'faith. Wisely, wisely.

83   Benvolio steps in as referee to stop the contest of wit before it becomes very rude!

84   **stop . . . hair**   stop my story just as I was getting to the point (with an obscene secondary meaning)

85   **tale large**   story indecent (with an obscene secondary meaning)

87   **whole depth**   end (with an obscene secondary meaning)

88   **occupy the argument**   continue the story (again, **occupy** had the sexual meaning of 'intercourse')

89   **goodly gear**   (i) good entertainment; (ii) entertaining clothing
Romeo is either referring back to their jesting, or he has caught sight of the Nurse.

91   **A shirt . . . smock**   a man and a woman

97   **God ye**   God grant you

98   **e'en**   evening (used for any time after noon)

102   **What a**   what sort of
Do you think the Nurse is really shocked by Mercutio's rude puns?

105   **troth**   faith, true word

106   **quoth 'a?**   did he say? (that is, indeed)
She is emphasising the truth of what Mercutio has just said about himself.

110   **fault**   lack

112   **took**   understood
Mercutio is sarcastic, as the Nurse has no idea what Mercutio is talking about.

How do you think the Nurse should be dressed for this scene? Draw a sketch for the costume design department.

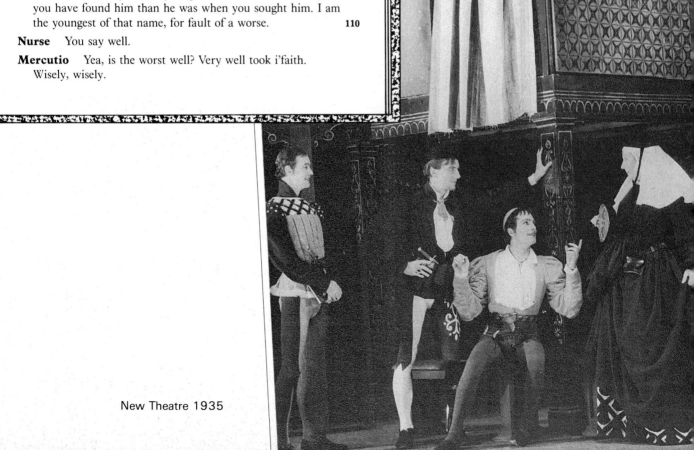

New Theatre 1935

114 **confidence** either a malapropism for 'conference', or a word used deliberately meaning 'confidential conversation'
Which do you think?
115 **endite** invite
116 **So ho** a hunter's cry when the quarry is sighted
118 **hare** punning on 'whore'
lenten pie a pie containing no meat and made during Lent
119 **hoar** stale (again, punning on 'whore')
spent used up
124 is not worth paying for
125 **hoars** (i) goes mouldy; (ii) goes whoring
126 **dinner** In Elizabethan times this meal was eaten around noon.
129 **lady, lady, lady** from an old ballad
How do you think Mercutio should say these lines?
130 **saucy merchant** insolent fellow
131 **ropery** joking
133 **stand to** abide by, live up to
135 **And** if
take him down cut him down to size
136 **Jacks** knaves
138 **flirt-gills** loose women
skains-mates cut-throat companions
139 **suffer** allow
140 **use ... pleasure** treat me as he will
In the following line Peter picks up an obscene secondary meaning which the Nurse does not intend.
142 **weapon** Again, Peter intends an obscene double-meaning.

Nurse If you be he sir, I desire some confidence with you.

Benvolio She will endite him to some supper.   115

Mercutio A bawd! A bawd! A bawd! So ho.

Romeo What hast thou found?

Mercutio No hare, sir, unless a hare, sir, in a lenten pie, that is something stale and hoar ere it be spent.

[He walks by them and sings]

An old hare hoar,   120
And an old hare hoar,
Is very good meat in Lent.
But a hare that is hoar
Is too much for a score
When it hoars ere it be spent.   125

Romeo, will you come to your father's? We'll to dinner thither.

Romeo I will follow you.

Mercutio Farewell, ancient lady, farewell, lady, lady, lady.

[Exeunt **Mercutio** *and* **Benvolio***]*

Nurse I pray you, sir, what saucy merchant was this, that was 130
so full of his ropery?

Romeo A gentleman, Nurse, that loves to hear himself talk, and will speak more in a minute than he will stand to in a month.

Nurse And 'a speak anything against me I'll take him down,   135
and 'a were lustier than he is, and twenty such Jacks. And if I cannot, I'll find those that shall. Scurvy knave! I am none of his flirt-gills, I am none of his skains-mates. *[She turns to* **Peter***, her servant]* And thou must stand by too and suffer every knave to use me at his pleasure!   140

Peter I saw no man use you at his pleasure; if I had, my weapon should quickly have been out. I warrant you, I dare draw as soon as another man, if I see occasion in a good quarrel, and the law on my side.

Nurse Now afore God I am so vexed that every part about   145

... if you should deal double with her ...

Temba Theatre Company 1988

me quivers. Scurvy knave. Pray you, sir, a word – and as I told you, my young lady bid me enquire you out. What she bid me say, I will keep to myself. But first let me tell ye, if ye should lead her in a fool's paradise, as they say, it were a very gross kind of behaviour, as they say; for the gentlewoman is young. And therefore, if you should deal double with her, truly it were an ill thing to be offered to any gentlewoman, and very weak dealing. 150

Romeo   Nurse, commend me to thy lady and mistress. I protest unto thee – 155

Nurse   Good heart, and i'faith I will tell her as much. Lord, Lord, she will be a joyful woman.

Romeo   What wilt thou tell her, Nurse? Thou dost not mark me.

Nurse   I will tell her, sir, that you do protest – which, as I take 160 it, is a gentlemanlike offer.

Romeo   Bid her devise
Some means to come to shrift this afternoon,
And there she shall at Friar Laurence' cell
Be shrived and married. Here is for thy pains. 165

Nurse   No truly, sir; not a penny.

Romeo   Go to, I say you shall.

Nurse   This afternoon, sir? Well, she shall be there.

Romeo   And stay, good Nurse, behind the abbey wall.
Within this hour my man shall be with thee, 170
And bring thee cords made like a tackled stair,
Which to the high topgallant of my joy
Must be my convoy in the secret night.
Farewell, be trusty, and I'll quit thy pains;
Farewell. Commend me to thy mistress. 175

Nurse   Now God in heaven bless thee. Hark you, sir.

Romeo   What say'st thou, my dear Nurse?

Nurse   Is your man secret? Did you ne'er hear say,
Two may keep counsel, putting one away?

Romeo   I warrant thee my man's as true as steel. 180

149 **in**   into
What kind of 'fool's paradise' do you think the Nurse means?
153 **weak**   contemptible
The Nurse probably means to say 'wicked'.
154 **commend me**   convey my best wishes to
156-7 The Nurse immediately takes **protest** in the usual Elizabethan sense of a declaration of love.
158 **mark**   pay attention to
163 **shrift**   confession
165 **shrived**   absolved (after confession)
pains   trouble
166-7 Do you think the Nurse takes any money?
171 **tackled stair**   rope ladder
172 **topgallant**   summit
The **topgallant** was the highest platform on a mast. What prompts Romeo to use this nautical image?
173 **convoy**   means of travel
174 **quit**   requit, reward
179 a proverb meaning that two people may keep a secret so long as a third is not involved
180 **warrant**   guarantee

Which part of this page is spoken in prose, and which in verse? Does this tell you anything about the characters and their mood?

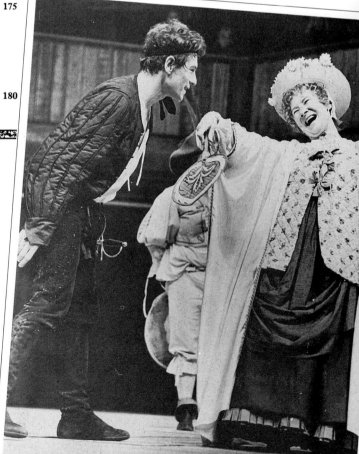

Decide which words from the text would provide the best caption to this photograph.

Royal Shakespeare Company 1976

182 **prating** chattering
What trait typical of the Nurse do we see in this line?
183 **fain . . . aboard** like to lay claim (to Juliet)
The image is of a guest in Elizabethan times who brought his own knife and laid it down on the table (or 'board') to lay claim to his place.
184 **as lief** rather
187 **clout** piece of cloth
versal universal, whole
rosemary a herb of remembrance associated with weddings, but also with funerals
Compare with Act IV Scene 5 line 79 and the stage direction following Act IV Scene 5 line 95.
188 **a** the same
190 **dog's name** 'R' resembles the growl of a dog. The Elizabethans probably sounded 'R' with a richer, more rolled sound than we do today.
– No Perhaps the Nurse was thinking of something rude.
192 **sententious** Probably the Nurse means 'sentences'.
197 go in front of me, and go quickly

3 **Perchance** perhaps
7 **Therefore** for this reason
nimble-pinioned swift-winged
Love the goddess Venus, to whom doves were sacred and whose chariot is represented as being drawn through the air by them
9 that is, it is noon and the sun is at its zenith
14 **bandy** strike
The metaphor is from tennis.
16 **feign as** pretend to be (perhaps she means that many old folks use their age as an excuse to move slowly)
What is ironic about this line in view of Juliet's later actions?

Imagine that you are impatiently waiting for news. Improvise the scene. (You could be on your own or with someone else who may be either very or not very sympathetic.)

Re-read lines 12–17, and then explain in your own words why Juliet considers the Nurse unsuited to her task.

Nurse   Well, sir, my mistress is the sweetest lady. Lord, Lord! When 'twas a little prating thing – O, there is a nobleman in town, one Paris, that would fain lay knife aboard; but she, good soul, had as lief see a toad, a very toad, as see him. I anger her sometimes and tell her that Paris is the properer **185** man, but I'll warrant you, when I say so she looks as pale as any clout in the versal world. Doth not rosemary and Romeo begin both with a letter?

Romeo   Ay, Nurse, what of that? Both with an 'R'.

Nurse   Ah, mocker! That's the dog's name, 'R' is for the – No, **190** I know it begins with some other letter; and she hath the prettiest sententious of it, of you and rosemary, that it would do you good to hear it.

Romeo   Commend me to thy lady.   [*Exit* **Romeo**]

Nurse   Ay, a thousand times. Peter!   **195**

Peter   Anon.

Nurse   Before, and apace.   [*Exeunt*]

Scene 5

Verona. Capulet's orchard. Enter **Juliet**.

Juliet   The clock struck nine when I did send the Nurse,
In half an hour she promised to return.
Perchance she cannot meet him. That's not so.
O, she is lame. Love's heralds should be thoughts
Which ten times faster glides than the sun's beams,   **5**
Driving back shadows over louring hills.
Therefore do nimble-pinioned doves draw Love,
And therefore hath the wind-swift Cupid wings.
Now is the sun upon the highmost hill
Of this day's journey, and from nine till twelve   **10**
Is three long hours, yet she is not come.
Had she affections and warm youthful blood
She would be as swift in motion as a ball:
My words would bandy her to my sweet love,
And his to me.   **15**
But old folks, many feign as they were dead –
Unwieldy, slow, heavy, and pale as lead.

Commend me to thy lady.
Bristol Old Vic 1975

[*Enter* **Nurse** *with* **Peter**]

O God she comes. O honey Nurse, what news?
Hast thou met with him? Send thy man away.

Nurse Peter, stay at the gate.   [*Exit* **Peter**] 20

Juliet Now good sweet Nurse – O Lord why look'st thou sad?
Though news be sad, yet tell them merrily,
If good, thou sham'st the music of sweet news
By playing it to me with so sour a face.

Nurse I am aweary, give me leave awhile.   25
Fie, how my bones ache. What a jaunce have I!

Juliet I would thou hadst my bones and I thy news.
Nay come, I pray thee, speak: good, good Nurse, speak.

Nurse Jesu, what haste. Can you not stay awhile?
Do you not see that I am out of breath?   30

Juliet How art thou out of breath when thou hast breath
To say to me that thou art out of breath?
The excuse that thou dost make in this delay
Is longer than the tale thou dost excuse.
Is thy news good or bad? Answer to that,   35
Say either, and I'll stay the circumstance.
Let me be satisfied: is't good or bad?

Nurse Well, you have made a simple choice. You know not
how to choose a man. Romeo? No, not he. Though his face
be better than any man's, yet his leg excels all men's, and for 40
a hand and a foot and a body, though they be not to be
talked on, yet they are past compare. He is not the flower of
courtesy, but I'll warrant him as gentle as a lamb. Go thy
ways, wench. Serve God. What, have you dined at home?

Juliet No, no. But all this did I know before.   45
What says he of our marriage? What of that?

Nurse Lord, how my head aches! What a head have I:
It beats as it would fall in twenty pieces.
My back a' t'other side – ah, my back, my back!
Beshrew your heart for sending me about   50
To catch my death with jauncing up and down.

Juliet I'faith, I am sorry that thou art not well.

---

22 To what does **them** refer, and why do you think it is pural?
26 **jaunce** jaunt
29 **stay awhile** wait a moment
33 **in** in making
34 **excuse** that is, excuse yourself from telling
36 **stay the cirumstance** wait for the details
38 **simple** silly
41-2 **to be talked on** worth talking about
42 **past compare** better than anything they could be compared with
43-4 **Go thy ways** enough of this
44 **Serve God** behave yourself
 What well now, tell me
48 **beats as** throbs as if
49 **a' t'** on the
50 **Beshrew your heart** bother you

Either analyse in detail how the Nurse teases Juliet during this episode; or improvise a scene where someone teases someone else by mischievously withholding good news for as long as possible.

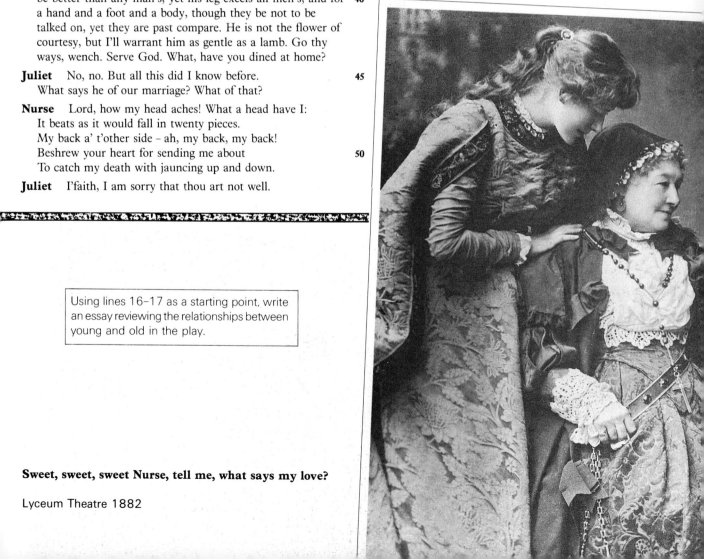

Using lines 16–17 as a starting point, write an essay reviewing the relationships between young and old in the play.

Sweet, sweet, sweet Nurse, tell me, what says my love?

Lyceum Theatre 1882

54 **honest** honourable, trustworthy
See line 77.
57 **within** inside
61 **Marry** by the Virgin Mary
come up, I trow an expression of impatience
64 **coil** fuss
65 **shrift** confession and absolution
67 **hie** hurry
68 **stays** awaits
69 What is happening to Juliet's face? Why do you
think the Nurse uses the epithet **wanton**?
71 **must** that is, must go
73 **a bird's nest** that is, to Juliet's bedroom
75 **bear** carry
burden (i) responsibility; (ii) weight (of a lover)
77 **high fortune** Fortune was often seen as a wheel.
When one's fortune was at the high point of the
wheel, there was only one way that it could go. Do
you think Juliet is aware of this irony?

1 **So...heavens** may the heavens so smile
Consider the irony of lines 1 and 2 in view of
subsequent events.
3 **come...can** whatever sorrow may come
4 **countervail** counteract
exchange of joy joy that I receive
6 **close** join (in marriage)

> Imagine you are either Romeo or Juliet.
> Describe your adventures from the time you
> first set eyes on Juliet/Romeo until your
> marriage.
>
> Why do you think the Nurse is so keen to
> play the part of bringing together Juliet and
> Romeo?

Bristol Old Vic 1983

Sweet, sweet, sweet Nurse, tell me, what says my love?

Nurse Your love says like an honest gentleman,
And a courteous, and a kind, and a handsome, 55
And I warrant a virtuous – Where is your mother?

Juliet Where is my mother? Why, she is within.
Where should she be? How oddly thou repliest.
'Your love says, like an honest gentleman,
"Where is your mother?"'

Nurse   O God's lady dear, 60
Are you so hot? Marry, come up, I trow.
Is this the poultice for my aching bones?
Henceforward do your messages yourself.

Juliet Here's such a coil. Come, what says Romeo?

Nurse Have you got leave to go to shrift today? 65

Juliet I have.

Nurse Then hie you hence to Friar Laurence' cell.
There stays a husband to make you a wife.
Now comes the wanton blood up in your cheeks.
They'll be in scarlet straight at any news. 70
Hie you to church. I must another way
To fetch a ladder by the which your love
Must climb a bird's nest soon when it is dark.
I am the drudge, and toil in your delight,
But you shall bear the burden soon at night. 75
Go. I'll to dinner. Hie you to the cell.

Juliet Hie to high fortune! Honest Nurse, farewell. [*Exeunt*]

Scene 6

Verona. Friar Laurence's cell. Enter **Friar Laurence** *and* **Romeo**.

Friar Laurence So smile the heavens upon this holy act
That after-hours with sorrow chide us not.

Romeo Amen, amen! But come what sorrow can,
It cannot countervail the exchange of joy
That one short minute gives me in her sight. 5
Do thou but close our hands with holy words,

**I am the drudge, and toil in your delight,
And you shall bear the burden soon at night.**

Then love-devouring death do what he dare:
It is enough I may but call her mine.

Friar Laurence   These violent delights have violent ends
And in their triumph die, like fire and powder,   10
Which as they kiss consume. The sweetest honey
Is loathsome in his own deliciousness,
And in the taste confounds the appetite.
Therefore love moderately; long love doth so.
Too swift arrives as tardy as too slow.   15

[*Enter* **Juliet**, *who runs to* **Romeo** *and embraces him*]

Here comes the lady. O, so light a foot
Will ne'er wear out the everlasting flint.
A lover may bestride the gossamers
That idles in the wanton summer air
And yet not fall; so light is vanity.   20

Juliet   Good even to my ghostly confessor.

Friar Laurence   Romeo shall thank thee, daughter, for us both.
                                               [**Romeo** *kisses her*]

Juliet   As much to him, else is his thanks too much.
                                               [*She returns the kiss*]

Romeo   Ah, Juliet, if the measure of thy joy
Be heaped like mine, and that thy skill be more   25
To blazon it, then sweeten with thy breath
This neighbour air, and let rich music's tongue
Unfold the imagined happiness that both
Receive in either by this dear encounter.

Juliet   Conceit, more rich in matter than in words,   30
Brags of his substance, not of ornament.
They are but beggars that can count their worth,
But my true love is grown to such excess
I cannot sum up sum of half my wealth.

Friar Laurence   Come, come with me and we will make
    short work   35
For, by your leaves, you shall not stay alone
Till holy church incorporate two in one.

                                                        [*Exeunt*]

8   **but**   simply
10 **triumph**   moment of explosion
        powder   gunpowder
12 **Is**   becomes (if too much is eaten)
13 **confounds**   spoils
14–15 Explain carefully the meaning of these lines. What is
        the point of the Friar's little sermon in lines 9–15?
18 **gossamers**   threads of a spider's web
19 **wanton**   playful
20 **light**   trivial, insubstantial
        vanity   fleeting earthly pleasures
22 that is, by kissing her
23 that is, she must give him another kiss if he is
        thanking her on behalf of the Friar and himself
24 **measure**   quantity
25 **that**   if
26 **blazon**   describe and proclaim
27 **neighbour**   surrounding
        rich music's tongue   that is, the music of your
        voice
28 **imagined**   inner, mental
30 **Conceit**   understanding
        matter   substance
31 is proud of sincere meaning, not mere impressive
        sounding words
32 **but**   nothing more than
34 **sum up sum**   add up the total

**You shall not stay alone
Till holy church incorporate two in one.**

Bristol Old Vic 1949

2 Capels Capulets
abroad about in the streets
3 'scape escape
4 It was supposed that people were more quarrelsome and that passions ran higher in hot weather and in hot climates. Is this true, do you think?
5 Why does Shakespeare change from Benvolio's verse to Mercutio's prose?
8 operation intoxicating effect
draw him draws his sword
drawer tavern servant who draws and serves the ale
10 Which word do you think Benvolio would emphasise in this line? See **eye** in line 20.
11 Jack knave
12 moved provoked
moody quarrelsome
13 moody to be moved quick to be provoked
15 and if
two such two such people
Explain the pun on 'two'.
20 hazel Explain Mercutio's pun.
22 meat food
addle rotten
26 doublet tight-fitting jacket
Sober clothes were appropriate for Lent, and new fashions were not appropriate until Easter. Why do you think the tailor was wearing his new creation early?
27 riband ribbon; that is, shoe-lace
28 tutor me from advise me against

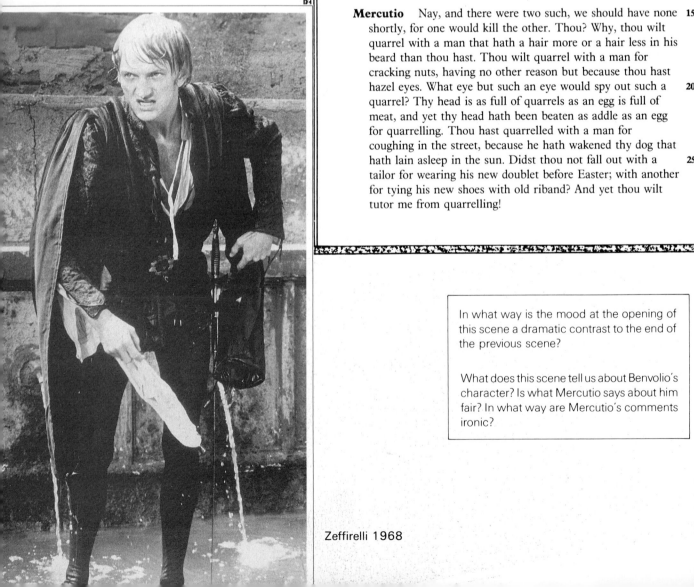

Zeffirelli 1968

Act III

Scene 1

Verona. A public place. Enter **Mercutio**, **Benvolio** *and* **Men**.

Benvolio   I pray thee, good Mercutio, let's retire;
The day is hot, the Capels are abroad,
And if we meet we shall not 'scape a brawl,
For now these hot days is the mad blood stirring.

Mercutio   Thou art like one of these fellows that, when he   5
enters the confines of a tavern, claps me his sword upon the table and says, 'God send me no need of thee!' and by the operation of the second cup draws him on the drawer, when indeed there is no need.

Benvolio   Am I like such a fellow?   10

Mercutio   Come, come, thou art as hot a Jack in thy mood as any in Italy; and as soon moved to be moody, and as soon moody to be moved.

Benvolio   And what to?

Mercutio   Nay, and there were two such, we should have none   15
shortly, for one would kill the other. Thou? Why, thou wilt quarrel with a man that hath a hair more or a hair less in his beard than thou hast. Thou wilt quarrel with a man for cracking nuts, having no other reason but because thou hast hazel eyes. What eye but such an eye would spy out such a   20
quarrel? Thy head is as full of quarrels as an egg is full of meat, and yet thy head hath been beaten as addle as an egg for quarrelling. Thou hast quarrelled with a man for coughing in the street, because he hath wakened thy dog that hath lain asleep in the sun. Didst thou not fall out with a   25
tailor for wearing his new doublet before Easter; with another for tying his new shoes with old riband? And yet thou wilt tutor me from quarrelling!

In what way is the mood at the opening of this scene a dramatic contrast to the end of the previous scene?

What does this scene tell us about Benvolio's character? Is what Mercutio says about him fair? In what way are Mercutio's comments ironic?

Benvolio   And I were so apt to quarrel as thou art, any man
should buy the fee simple of my life for an hour and a   **30**
quarter.

Mercutio   The fee simple! O simple!

[*Enter **Tybalt** and **others***]

Benvolio   By my head, here comes the Capulets.

Mercutio   By my heel, I care not.

Tybalt   Follow me close, for I will speak to them.   **35**
Gentlemen, good e'en: a word with one of you.

Mercutio   And but one word with one of us? Couple it with
something, make it a word and a blow.

Tybalt   You shall find me apt enough to that, sir, and you
will give me occasion.   **40**

Mercutio   Could you not take some occasion without giving?

Tybalt   Mercutio, thou consortest with Romeo.

Mercutio   Consort? What, dost thou make us minstrels? And
thou make minstrels of us, look to hear nothing but discords.
Here's my fiddlestick, here's that shall make you dance.   **45**
Zounds, consort!

Benvolio   We talk here in the public haunt of men.
Either withdraw unto some private place,
Or reason coldly of your grievances,
Or else depart. Here all eyes gaze on us.   **50**

Mercutio   Men's eyes were made to look, and let them gaze.
I will not budge for no man's pleasure, I.

[*Enter **Romeo***]

Tybalt   Well, peace be with you, sir, here comes my man.

Mercutio   But I'll be hanged, sir, if he wear your livery.
Marry, go before to field, he'll be your follower.   **55**
Your worship in that sense may call him 'man'.

30–1 buy . . . quarter that is, I would not live longer
than an hour and a quarter (**fee simple** means
complete legal ownership)

32 O simple! What an utterly weak joke!

34 heel the most scornful reply that he can think of,
perhaps with the suggestion that he will not 'take to
his heels' and run away

35 Note the return to verse for two lines. What is the
effect of the mixture of prose and verse in the
episode which follows?
To whom is Tybalt talking in this line?

36 e'en evening (used any time after midday in
Elizabethan England)

37 And but only

40 occasion excuse, reason
Tybalt is keeping to the strict rules of duelling.

41 without giving without being given an excuse

42 consortest are often in the company of

43 Consort! Mercutio deliberately takes this in the
sense of a group of musicians, who were regarded
as servants; and thus, as a gentleman, he can find
an **occasion** for a quarrel in response to an
apparent insult.

45 fiddlestick To what do you think Mercutio refers?
Find other puns on fencing and music in Act II
Scene 4.

46 Zounds by God's wounds

49 coldly calmly, without heat

53 my man my chosen opponent

54 your livery the colours and uniform worn by your
servants
Mercutio deliberately interprets **man** in the previous
line as 'manservant'.

55 Marry by the Virgin Mary
Mercutio says that the only sense in which Tybalt
can claim Romeo as his 'man' is that Romeo will
follow him to wherever he wishes to fight (**field**
means 'dwelling-place')

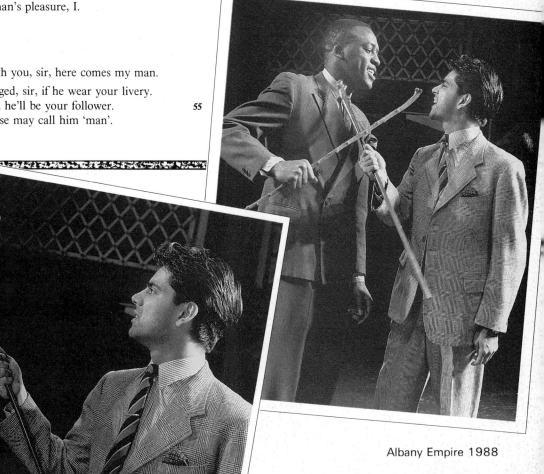

Albany Empire 1988

57 bear feel for
Tybalt is, of course, being sarcastic.
afford offer
58 villain implying (i) low behaviour; (ii) low birth
Under normal circumstances the insulted man would have immediately demanded satisfaction in a duel. His honour would demand it.
59–61 It is dramatically ironic that only Romeo and the audience understand the significance of these words.
60 the appertaining rage the (lack of) appropriate anger in response
63 Boy Where has this insulting term already been applied to Tybalt himself?
What do you think Tybalt means by **this**?
66 devise imagine
68 tender value
70 Why is Mercutio now so angry?
71 Alla stoccata an Italian fencing term meaning 'at the thrust'
Mercutio is contemptuous of this new jargon, and uses the phrase as a nick-name for Tybalt.
carries it away gets away with it, carries (wins) the day
72 Why **rat-catcher**? (Read ahead. See also Act II Scene 4 line 18.)
walk that is, to the duelling-place
74–5 nine lives Cats are supposed to have nine lives.
75 withal with
Mercutio is saying that he intends to take one of his lives.
75–6 as you . . . hereafter depending on how you treat me after this time
76 dry-beat cudgel, thrash
Mercutio implies that in future he will beat him like a low fellow rather than offer him the honour of duelling like a gentleman.
77 pilcher scabbard
78 mine . . . it my sword . . . your sword
79 I accept your challenge
81 passado thrust (see Act II Scene 4 lines 23–4)
Mercutio continues to mock Tybalt's fencing jargon.
83 forbear cease, stop
85 bandying sword play
89 sped done for

Does everyone at first realise the seriousness of Mercutio's wound? How would you direct that part of the scene?

Re-read lines 88–113. Give instructions to the actor playing Romeo, explaining how his attitudes change during this extract.

Tybalt   Romeo, the love I bear thee can afford
No better term than this: thou art a villain.

Romeo   Tybalt, the reason that I have to love thee
Doth much excuse the appertaining rage   60
To such a greeting: villain am I none,
Therefore farewell. I see thou knowest me not.

Tybalt   Boy, this shall not excuse the injuries
That thou hast done me, therefore turn and draw.

Romeo   I do protest I never injured thee,   65
But love thee better than thou canst devise
Till thou shalt know the reason of my love.
And so, good Capulet, which name I tender
As dearly as mine own, be satisfied.

Mercutio   O calm, dishonourable, vile submission: 70
Alla stoccata carries it away!   [*He draws*]
Tybalt, you rat-catcher, will you walk?

Tybalt   What wouldst thou have with me?

Mercutio   Good King of Cats, nothing but one of your nine
lives. That I mean to make bold withal, and, as you shall use   75
me hereafter, dry-beat the rest of the eight. Will you pluck
your sword out of his pilcher by the ears? Make haste, lest
mine be about your ears ere it be out.

Tybalt   I am for you.   [*He draws*]

Romeo   Gentle Mercutio, put thy rapier up.   80

Mercutio   Come sir, your passado.   [*They fight*]

Romeo   Draw, Benvolio, beat down their weapons.
Gentlemen, for shame, forbear this outrage.
Tybalt, Mercutio! The Prince expressly hath
Forbid this bandying in Verona streets.   85
Hold, Tybalt! Good Mercutio!

[**Tybalt** *under Romeo's arm thrusts* **Mercutio** *in*]

A Follower   Away Tybalt.   [*Exit* **Tybalt**, *with his* **followers**]

Mercutio   I am hurt.
A plague o' both your houses. I am sped.

I am for you.

Citizens Theatre 1975

Is he gone, and hath nothing?

Benvolio   What, art thou hurt?   90

Mercutio   Ay, ay, a scratch, a scratch. Marry, 'tis enough.
Where is my page? Go villain, fetch a surgeon.

*[Exit **Page**]*

Romeo   Courage, man, the hurt cannot be much.

Mercutio   No, 'tis not so deep as a well, nor so wide as a
church door, but 'tis enough, 'twill serve. Ask for me   95
tomorrow and you shall find me a grave man. I am
peppered, I warrant, for this world. A plague o' both your
houses. Zounds, a dog, a rat, a mouse, a cat, to scratch a
man to death. A braggart, a rogue, a villain, that fights by
the book of arithmetic – why the devil came you between   100
us? I was hurt under your arm.

Romeo   I thought all for the best.

Mercutio   Help me into some house, Benvolio,
Or I shall faint. A plague o' both your houses,
They have made worms' meat of me.   105
I have it, and soundly too. Your houses!

*[Exit **Mercutio**, with **Benvolio**]*

Romeo   This gentleman, the Prince's near ally,
My very friend, hath got this mortal hurt
In my behalf – my reputation stained
With Tybalt's slander – Tybalt that an hour   110
Hath been my cousin. O sweet Juliet,
Thy beauty hath made me effeminate
And in my temper softened valour's steel.

*[Enter **Benvolio**]*

Benvolio   O Romeo, Romeo, brave Mercutio is dead,
That gallant spirit hath aspired the clouds   115
Which too untimely here did scorn the earth.

Romeo   This day's black fate on mo days doth depend:
This but begins the woe others must end.

90 **hath nothing** without a scratch
91 **scratch** Mercutio, although dying, still plays on words. How is this word appropriate to a wound received from Tybalt?
Can you spot a pun in Mercutio's next speech? Is the pun appropriate, given the seriousness of the situation?
92 **villain** fellow
As Mercutio addresses this to his servant, there is no insult intended.
95 **serve** be sufficient (to kill him)
97 **peppered** finished (because I have a hole in me)
warrant guarantee
100 **book of arithmetic** fencing manual, which prescribes rules through numbers and diagrams See Act II Scene 4 line 20.
105 **worm's meat** because maggots eat corpses (a common image in Shakespeare)
106 **it** a death-wound See Act II Scene 4 line 24.
107 **near ally** close relative
108 **very** true
109 **In** on
110 **Tybalt's slander** See lines 57–64.
an hour for an hour
To what is Romeo referring?
111 **cousin** relative
113 **temper** temperament; also referring to the process used for the hardening of steel
115 **aspired** climbed up to
116 **untimely** prematurely, before his time (on earth) was naturally finished
scorn reject
117 **mo** move
depend have an impact
118 **but** only

Courage, man, the hurt cannot be much.

Bristol Old Vic 1966

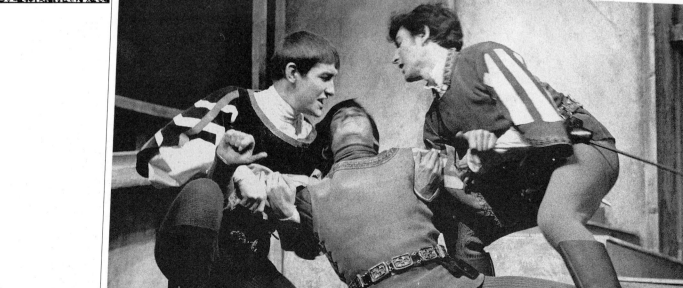

SD Instead of having Tybalt return, the 1968 Zeffirelli film version has Romeo chasing after Tybalt (with line 119, among others, cut). Why do you think this change was made? Is a different interpretation created? Remember that film and stage are different media.

121 respective lenity considerate mildness
Romeo starts to talk like a typical Elizabethan stage revenger.

122 conduct guide

123 To what is Romeo referring?

124 late recently

126 Staying waiting

128 boy . . . consort See lines 42 and 63.

129 This To what do you think Romeo is referring?

131 up aroused, in the streets

134 fool plaything, victim of a cruel joke

137 Why does the officer say 'Up' to Benvolio?

140 discover reveal

141 manage conduct

What do you think are the advantages and disadvantages of integrated casting (that is, using people from different ethnic groups in the same production)?

Left: Royal Shakespeare Company 1986; right: Young Vic 1987–8

[*Enter* **Tybalt**]

Benvolio   Here comes the furious Tybalt back again.

Romeo   Again, in triumph, and Mercutio slain.   120
   Away to heaven respective lenity,
   And fire-eyed fury be my conduct now!
   Now, Tybalt, take the 'villain' back again
   That late thou gav'st me, for Mercutio's soul
   Is but a little way above our heads,   125
   Staying for thine to keep him company.
   Either thou, or I, or both must go with him.

Tybalt   Thou wretched boy, that didst consort him here,
   Shalt with him hence.

Romeo   This shall determine that.
                                   [*They fight.* **Tybalt** *falls*]

Benvolio   Romeo, away, be gone!   130
   The citizens are up, and Tybalt slain!
   Stand not amazed, the Prince will doom thee death
   If thou art taken. Hence, be gone, away!

Romeo   O, I am fortune's fool.

Benvolio   Why dost thou stay?

                                   [*Exit* **Romeo**. *Enter* **Officers**]

Officer   Which way ran he that killed Mercutio?   135
   Tybalt, that murderer, which way ran he?

Benvolio   There lies that Tybalt.

Officer   Up, sir, go with me.
   I charge thee in the Prince's name obey.

[*Enter* **Prince**, **Montague**, **Capulet**, *their* **Wives** *and* **All**]

Prince   Where are the vile beginners of this fray?

Benvolio   O noble Prince, I can discover all   140
   The unlucky manage of this fatal brawl.
   There lies the man, slain by young Romeo,
   That slew thy kinsman brave Mercutio.

Lady Capulet   Tybalt, my cousin, O my brother's child!
O Prince, O husband, O, the blood is spilled   145
Of my dear kinsman. Prince, as thou art true,
For blood of ours shed blood of Montague.
O cousin, cousin.

Prince   Benvolio, who began this bloody fray?

Benvolio   Tybalt, here slain, whom Romeo's hand did slay.   150
Romeo, that spoke him fair, bid him bethink
How nice the quarrel was, and urged withal
Your high displeasure. All this uttered
With gentle breath, calm look, knees humbly bowed,
Could not take truce with the unruly spleen   155
Of Tybalt, deaf to peace, but that he tilts
With piercing steel at bold Mercutio's breast,
Who, all as hot, turns deadly point to point
And, with a martial scorn, with one hand beats
Cold death aside, and with the other sends   160
It back to Tybalt, whose dexterity
Retorts it. Romeo, he cries aloud
'Hold, friends! Friends part!' and swifter than his tongue
His agile arm beats down their fatal points
And 'twixt them rushes; underneath whose arm   165
An envious thrust from Tybalt hit the life
Of stout Mercutio; and then Tybalt fled,
But by and by comes back to Romeo,
Who had but newly entertained revenge,
And to't they go like lightning: for, ere I   170
Could draw to part them, was stout Tybalt slain,
And as he fell did Romeo turn and fly.
This is the truth, or let Benvolio die.

Lady Capulet   He is a kinsman to the Montague.
Affection makes him false. He speaks not true.   175
Some twenty of them fought in this black strife
And all those twenty could but kill one life.
I beg for justice, which thou, Prince, must give.
Romeo slew Tybalt. Romeo must not live.

Prince   Romeo slew him, he slew Mercutio.   180

---

151   **him fair**   pleasantly to him
      bethink   think about, consider
152   **nice**   petty
      withal   with it, in addition
155   **take truce**   make peace
      spleen   ill-temper (it was supposed that anger was
      generated in the spleen)
159– **with one hand . . . to Tybalt**   They are fighting
61   with sword in one hand and dagger in the other.
162   **Retorts it**   turns back **cold death** (that is, the
      thrust of the steel)
165   **'twixt**   between
166   **envious**   malicious
168   **by and by**   very soon
169   **entertained**   accepted thoughts of
176–7 From where, do you suppose, has Lady Capulet
      received her account of the fray? Is it accurate?

Why do you think Benvolio mentions the
fact that Mercutio was the Prince's kinsman
(line 143)? How is Benvolio's role here
similar to that in Act I Scene 1? Is Benvolio's
account of the fray strictly accurate? (See
line 175.)

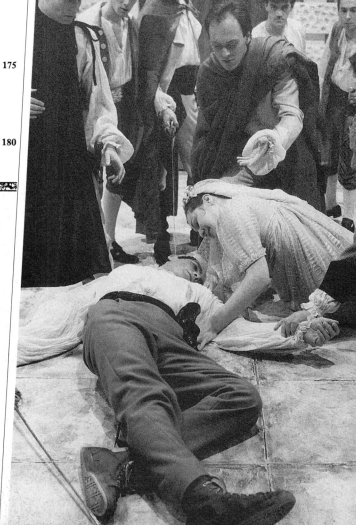

Tybalt, my cousin, O my brother's child!

Bristol Old Vic 1983

183–4 His fault . . . Tybalt Montague may be correct, but he would know that the lawless times had long since passed when it was acceptable for a man to take the law into his own hands (as in certain circumstances by Anglo-Saxon England). The Prince's punishment emphasises the point.

187 Mercutio is a kinsman.

188 amerce punish

191 Nor . . . nor neither . . . nor
purchase out buy off the penalty for

194 What is the dramatic impact of leaving Tybalt's body onstage until this point?

195 but only
In what sense does the Prince see mercy, in this case, causing more murder?

1–4 The sun (Phoebus) was traditionally seen as a chariot drawn by horses. Phaeton, permitted to drive the chariot of his father Apollo for one day, allowed the horses to career recklessly.

1 apace at a great pace

2 lodging resting place (the west)

5 close enclosing (and thus ensuring privacy)

6 runaway's . . . wink Editors disagree as to the meaning of this. Any ideas?

9 if . . . blind See Act I Scene 1 line 167.

10 civil sober (because black)

12 lose . . . match a paradox in that she will lose her virginity in winning her husband

13 stainless that is, the lovers are innocent, without blot or stain

Who now the price of his dear blood doth owe?

Montague   Not Romeo, Prince, he was Mercutio's friend;
His fault concludes but what the law should end,
The life of Tybalt.

Prince   And for that offence
Immediately we do exile him hence.   **185**
I have an interest in your hearts' proceeding;
My blood for your rude brawls doth lie a-bleeding.
But I'll amerce you with so strong a fine
That you shall all repent the loss of mine.
I will be deaf to pleading and excuses;   **190**
Nor tears nor prayers shall purchase out abuses.
Therefore use none. Let Romeo hence in haste,
Else, when he is found, that hour is his last.
Bear hence this body, and attend our will.
Mercy but murders, pardoning those that kill.   **195**

[*Exeunt*]

Scene 2

Verona. Capulet's house. Enter **Juliet** *alone.*

Juliet   Gallop apace, you fiery-footed steeds,
Towards Phoebus' lodging. Such a waggoner
As Phaeton would whip you to the west
And bring in cloudy night immediately.
Spread thy close curtain, love-performing night,   **5**
That runaway's eyes may wink, and Romeo
Leap to these arms untalked-of and unseen.
Lovers can see to do their amorous rites
By their own beauties; or, if love be blind,
It best agrees with night. Come, civil night,   **10**
Thou sober-suited matron, all in black,
And learn me how to lose a winning match
Played for a pair of stainless maidenhoods.

Say briefly but clearly in what ways Act III Scene 1 is a turning point in the action of the play.

Consider the poetic qualities of lines 1–31.

Comment on the dramatic and ironic contrast between the end of Scene 1 and the opening of Scene 2.

Ellen Terry as Juliet, Lyceum Theatre, London, 1882

Hood my unmanned blood, bating in my cheeks,
With thy black mantle, till strange love grow bold,   15
Think true love acted simple modesty.
Come night, come Romeo, come thou day in night,
For thou wilt lie upon the wings of night
Whiter than new snow upon a raven's back.
Come gentle night, come loving black-browed night,   20
Give me my Romeo; and when I shall die
Take him and cut him out in little stars,
And he will make the face of heaven so fine
That all the world will be in love with night,
And pay no worship to the garish sun.   25
O, I have bought the mansion of a love
But not possessed it, and though I am sold,
Not yet enjoyed. So tedious is this day
As is the night before some festival
To an impatient child that hath new robes   30
And may not wear them. O, here comes my Nurse.

[*Enter* **Nurse** *with cords, wringing her hands*]

And she brings news, and every tongue that speaks
But Romeo's name speaks heavenly eloquence.
Now, Nurse, what news? What hast thou there?
The cords that Romeo bid thee fetch?

Nurse   Ay, ay, the cords.   35

Juliet   Ay me, what news? Why dost thou wring thy hands?

Nurse   Ah weraday, he's dead, he's dead, he's dead!
We are undone, lady, we are undone!
Alack the day, he's gone, he's killed, he's dead!

Juliet   Can heaven be so envious?

Nurse   Romeo can,   40
Though heaven cannot. O Romeo, Romeo,
Who ever would have thought it? Romeo!

Juliet   What devil art thou that dost torment me thus?
This torture should be roared in dismal hell.
Hath Romeo slain himself? Say thou but 'Ay'   45

14–15 The imagery is from falconry.
     unmanned means 'untrained' in falconry, as Juliet is yet without husband. As the fluttering wings of a falcon is subdued by having a hood placed over the bird's head, so night will **Hood** Juliet and cover (by **bating**) her blushing cheeks.
15 **strange** unfamiliar
     mantle cloak
16 that is, the act of love will come to be thought of as proper and genuine modesty
17 **night** What pun do you think Juliet might intend here?
     day in night Romeo will shine out like day against the night.
25 **garish** gaudy, unsubtle (because the starlight of Romeo at night will be so much more delightful)
26–8 **O, I have . . . enjoyed** Juliet sees the possession of her love as the buying of a house which she has not yet lived in; she is also **sold**, although possession (that is sexually) has not yet taken place.
30 **impatient child** How does this homely image differ from the imagery elsewhere in Juliet's speech?
35 **cords** rope-ladder
     Why has the Nurse brought it?
37 **weraday** alas
40 **envious** spiteful
     Romeo can that is, Romeo can be so malicious
44 **torture** To what does Juliet refer?
45–50 Repeated punning, even in a tragic situation, was common in Elizabethan literature. (See Mercutio's use of **grave** in line 96 of the previous scene.) These lines are complicated, but can be unravelled. Working in groups, see if you can work out their meaning.

We are undone, lady, we are undone!

Bristol Old Vic 1975

47 **cockatrice** It was reputed that this legendary creature, sometimes called the 'basilk', could kill by its look.
48 **not I** as good as dead
49 **those eyes shut** that is, Romeo's (because dead)
51 **sounds** that is, words
determine of decide about
weal well-being
52 The Nurse continues with 'I' sounds.
53 a common expression of apology for mentioning something disagreeable
For what do you think the Nurse may be apologising?
54 **corse** corpse
56 What does Juliet still think? And why may her heart be 'bankrupt'?
59 **Vile earth** that is, her body
to earth to the grave
motion physical movement
62 **honest** honourable
64 **contrary** in an opposite direction
67 **dreadful ... doom** the trumpet which, according to the Bible, will announce the end of the world. (See I Corinthians, 15:52.)
73–85 Juliet here laments the contrast between appearance and reality in a series of paradoxes and oxymorons (a phrase which contains opposing qualities; for instance, **fiend angelical**).
73 Satan was sometimes pictured as appearing to Eve as a serpent with a human face and amid flowers. This image was a popular one, and was used by Shakespeare in at least three other plays.
hid with hidden by
76 **keep** guard
By tradition, dragons guarded caves which contained treasure.
78 **Just ... justly** exact ... exactly
81 **bower** hide (as in a beautiful arbour)

And that bare vowel 'I' shall poison more
Than the death-darting eye of cockatrice.
I am not I if there be such an 'I',
Or those eyes shut that makes thee answer 'Ay'.
If he be slain say 'Ay', or if not, 'No'.   50
Brief sounds determine of my weal or woe.

Nurse   I saw the wound, I saw it with mine eyes
– God save the mark – here on his manly breast.
A piteous corse, a bloody piteous corse,
Pale, pale as ashes, all bedaubed in blood,   55
All in gore-blood. I swounded at the sight.

Juliet   O break, my heart. Poor bankrupt, break at once.
To prison, eyes, ne'er look on liberty.
Vile earth to earth resign, end motion here,
And thou and Romeo press one heavy bier.   60

Nurse   O Tybalt, Tybalt, the best friend I had.
O courteous Tybalt, honest gentleman.
That ever I should live to see thee dead.

Juliet   What storm is this that blows so contrary?
Is Romeo slaughtered and is Tybalt dead?   65
My dearest cousin, and my dearer lord?
Then dreadful trumpet sound the general doom,
For who is living if those two are gone?

Nurse   Tybalt is gone and Romeo banished.
Romeo that killed him, he is banished.   70

Juliet   O God! Did Romeo's hand shed Tybalt's blood?

Nurse   It did, it did, alas the day, it did.

Juliet   O serpent heart, hid with a flowering face.
Did ever dragon keep so fair a cave?
Beautiful tyrant, fiend angelical,   75
Dove-feathered raven, wolvish-ravening lamb!
Despised substance of divinest show!
Just opposite to what thou justly seem'st!
A damned saint, an honourable villain!
O nature what hadst thou to do in hell   80
When thou didst bower the spirit of a fiend

The image of a serpent concealing itself under a plant was a popular one, and is used by Shakespeare several times in his plays. See note to line 73.

Woodcut from Geoffrey Whitney, *A Choice of Emblemes*, 1586

In mortal paradise of such sweet flesh?
Was ever book containing such vile matter
So fairly bound? O, that deceit should dwell
In such a gorgeous palace.

Nurse   There's no trust,   85
No faith, no honesty in men. All perjured,
All forsworn, all naught, all dissemblers.
Ah, where's my man? Give me some aqua-vitae.
These griefs, these woes, these sorrows make me old.
Shame come to Romeo.

Juliet   Blistered be thy tongue   90
For such a wish. He was not born to shame.
Upon his brow shame is ashamed to sit,
For 'tis a throne where honour may be crowned
Sole monarch of the universal earth.
O, what a beast was I to chide at him.   95

Nurse   Will you speak well of him that killed your cousin?

Juliet   Shall I speak ill of him that is my husband?
Ah, poor my lord, what tongue shall smooth thy name
When I thy three-hours wife have mangled it?
But wherefore, villain, didst thou kill my cousin?   100
That villain cousin would have killed my husband.
Back, foolish tears, back to your native spring;
Your tributary drops belong to woe
Which you mistaking offer up to joy.
My husband lives, that Tybalt would have slain,   105
And Tybalt's dead, that would have slain my husband.
All this is comfort. Wherefore weep I then?
Some word there was, worser than Tybalt's death,
That murdered me. I would forget it fain,
But O, it presses to my memory   110
Liked damned guilty deeds to sinners' minds.
Tybalt is dead and Romeo – banished.
That 'banished', that one word 'banished',
Hath slain ten thousand Tybalts: Tybalt's death
Was woe enough, if it had ended there.   115
Or if sour woe delights in fellowship

82 **mortal paradise** Juliet is probably comparing Romeo to the Garden of Eden, and the serpent within it.
83 **book** See the imagery used by Lady Capulet in Act I Scene 3 lines 77–8.
86 **perjured** oath-breakers
87 **forsworn** liars
   naught wicked
   dissemblers deceivers
88 **aqua-vitae** brandy (or other strong drink) from the Latin meaning 'water of life'
85-90 Which two of the Nurse's characteristics can we deduce from this speech of hers?
90-9 Why do you think Juliet talks to the Nurse in this way after what she herself has said?
90 **Blistered be thy tongue** It was supposed that slander caused blisters on the tongue.
98 **poor my** my poor (this is called a 'transferred adjective')
   smooth thy name heal your reputation
99 In what sense is Juliet the **three-hours wife** of Romeo?
100 **wherefore** why, for what reason
102 **native spring** natural source
103 **tributary drops** tear drops which are as tribute Juliet is saying that tears belong to unhappiness, as she is now happy because Romeo is alive.
105 **that** whom
106 **that would have slain** who wished to kill
109 **fain** gladly
110, **to** upon
111
111 **damned guilty deeds** deeds worthy of damnation
114 **Hath slain** is equivalent to the killing of
116 **fellowship** companionship

Decide where in Act III Scene 2 each of these moments occur.
Add captions if you wish.

Temba Theatre Company 1988

117 needly will be ranked needs to be accompanied by
120 modern ordinary (because the death of a father or mother could be seen as happening in the natural cause of events)
121 rearward rearguard (suggesting a surprise attack from behind, and possibly with a play on 'rear-word')
123 Is is as if to say
126 that word's death the extent of death implied in that word (**banished**)
sound (i) give adequate expression to; (ii) find the bottom of
132 beguiled tricked
138 Hie hurry
139 wot know
140 Hark listen

1 fearful full of fear
2 suffering is attracted to you
2–3 In what sense are these lines ironic?

In groups of three, decide who should play Juliet, who the Nurse, and who should be director. Rehearse speeches from Scene 2, taking especial care over how you think particular lines should be spoken and which words/syllables should be stressed.

Re-read lines 73–126 of Scene 2. Consider (a) presentation of characters, (b) dramatic interest, and (c) poetic qualities.

And needly will be ranked with other griefs,
Why followed not, when she said 'Tybalt's dead',
Thy father or thy mother, nay or both,
Which modern lamentation might have moved?　　120
But with a rearward following Tybalt's death,
'Romeo is banished': to speak that word
Is father, mother, Tybalt, Romeo, Juliet,
All slain, all dead. Romeo is banished,
There is no end, no limit, measure, bound,　　125
In that word's death. No words can that woe sound.
Where is my father and my mother, Nurse?

Nurse　Weeping and wailing over Tybalt's corse.
Will you go to them? I will bring you thither.

Juliet　Wash they his wounds with tears? Mine shall be spent　130
When theirs are dry, for Romeo's banishment.
Take up those cords. Poor ropes, you are beguiled,
Both you and I, for Romeo is exiled.
He made you for a highway to my bed,
But I, a maid, die maiden-widowed.　　135
Come, cords, come, Nurse, I'll to my wedding bed,
And death, not Romeo take my maidenhead.

Nurse　Hie to your chamber. I'll find Romeo
To comfort you. I wot well where he is.
Hark ye, your Romeo will be here at night.　　140
I'll to him. He is hid at Laurence' cell.

Juliet　O find him, give this ring to my true knight
And bid him come to take his last farewell.
　　　　　　　　　　　　　　　　　　[*Exeunt*]

Scene 3

Friar Laurence's cell. Enter **Friar Laurence**.

Friar Laurence　Romeo, come forth, come forth, thou fearful man.
Affliction is enamoured of thy parts
And thou art wedded to calamity.

[*Enter* **Romeo**]

Zeffirelli 1968

How does Shakespeare hint at the likely location of Scene 3? Bear in mind that there were few stage settings in the Elizabethan theatre.

Romeo   Father, what news? What is the Prince's doom?
What sorrow craves acquaintance at my hand   5
That I yet know not?

Friar Laurence   Too familiar
Is my dear son with such sour company.
I bring thee tidings of the Prince's doom.

Romeo   What less than doomsday is the Prince's doom?

Friar Laurence   A gentler judgement vanished from his lips: 10
Not body's death but body's banishment.

Romeo   Ha! Banishment! Be merciful, say 'death'.
For exile hath more terror in his look,
Much more than death. Do not say 'banishment'.

Friar Laurence   Hence from Verona art thou banished.   15
Be patient, for the world is broad and wide.

Romeo   There is no world without Verona walls
But purgatory, torture, hell itself;
Hence 'banished' is banished from the world,
And world's exile is death. Then 'banished'   20
Is death, mistermed. Calling death 'banished'
Thou cut'st my head off with a golden axe
And smilest upon the stroke that murders me.

Friar Laurence   O deadly sin, O rude unthankfulness.
Thy fault our law calls death, but the kind Prince,   25
Taking thy part, hath rushed aside the law
And turned that black word 'death' to banishment.
This is dear mercy and thou seest it not.

Romeo   'Tis torture and not mercy. Heaven is here
Where Juliet lives, and every cat and dog   30
And little mouse, every unworthy thing,
Live here in heaven and may look on her,
But Romeo may not. More validity,
More honourable state, more courtship lives
In carrion flies than Romeo. They may seize   35
On the white wonder of dear Juliet's hand
And steal immortal blessing from her lips,
Who, even in pure and vestal modesty

4	**doom**	sentence
9	**doomsday**	that is, death
10	**vanished**	escaped into the air
16	What consolation is Friar Laurence trying to offer Romeo?	
17	**without**	outside
20	**world's exile is**	exile from the world is the same as
21	**mistermed**	call by the wrong name
21–3	**Calling death . . . murders me**	What comment is Romeo making on the comfort which the Friar is trying to give him?
25	**calls**	judges worthy of
26	**rushed**	thrust
28	**dear**	precious because unusual
29	Notice how the natural stress of the iambic pentameter places an emphasis on **here**.	
33	**validity**	value, worthiness
34	**state**	status, rank
	courtship	courtly behaviour (with a pun on 'court' meaning 'woo')
35	**carrion flies**	flies which feed upon corpses
36	Find a place in Act I Scene 5 where Romeo refers to Juliet's hand.	
38	**vestal**	maidenlike

> Compare Romeo's behaviour with that of Juliet in the previous scene. Look closely at the language used to illustrate their states of mind.

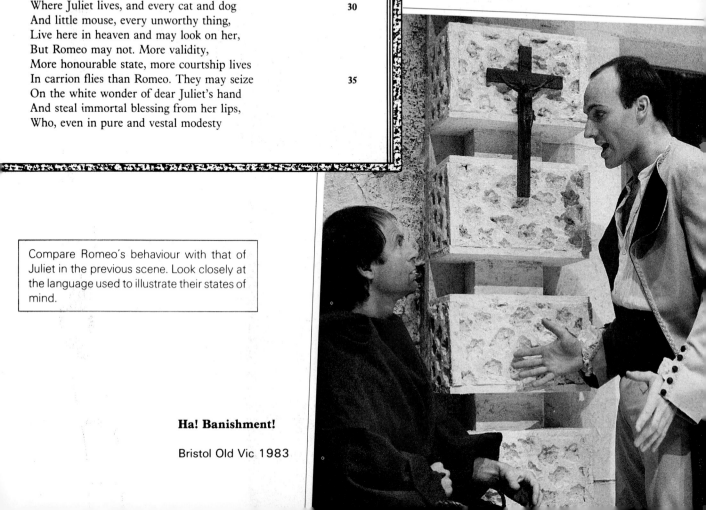

Ha! Banishment!

Bristol Old Vic 1983

39   continually blush, as if thinking the touching of one lip by the other to be a sin
In simple language, what quality is Romeo seeing in Juliet's lips?
41   **fly**   run away
44   **poison**   What knowledge of the Friar (later to prove fatal) does Romeo remind us of?
45   **mean . . . mean**   method . . . low, base
47   In what sense do you think the damned in hell might see themselves as 'banished'?
49   **divine**   holy man
     ghostly   spiritual
52   **fond**   foolish
55   a philosophical attitude, which helps to soothe adversity
59   **Displant**   transplant
63   **dispute . . . estate**   discuss your situation with you
66   **An hour but married**   married only one hour
67   **Doting**   love-sick
70   Explain Romeo's metaphor here.
73   **infold**   enfolds, hides

Imagine you are trying to console a friend who feels that nobody has ever been in the same trouble before (see lines 64–70). Write a dialogue or improvise in pairs.

Still blush, as thinking their own kisses sin.
But Romeo may not, he is banished.   40
Flies may do this, but I from this must fly.
They are free men but I am banished.
And sayest thou yet that exile is not death?
Hadst thou no poison mixed, no sharp-ground knife,
No sudden mean of death, though ne'er so mean,   45
But 'banished' to kill me? 'Banished'?
O Friar, the damned use that word in hell.
Howling attends it. How hast thou the heart,
Being a divine, a ghostly confessor,
A sin-absolver, and my friend professed,   50
To mangle me with that word 'banished'?

Friar Laurence   Thou fond mad man, hear me a little speak.

Romeo   O, thou wilt speak again of banishment.

Friar Laurence   I'll give thee armour to keep off that word,
Adversity's sweet milk, philosophy,   55
To comfort thee though thou art banished.

Romeo   Yet 'banished'? Hang up philosophy!
Unless philosophy can make a Juliet,
Displant a town, reverse a Prince's doom,
It helps not, it prevails not. Talk no more.   60

Friar Laurence   O, then I see that mad men have no ears.

Romeo   How should they when that wise men have no eyes?

Friar Laurence   Let me dispute with thee of thy estate.

Romeo   Thou canst not speak of that thou dost not feel.
Wert thou as young as I, Juliet thy love,   65
An hour but married, Tybalt murdered,
Doting like me, and like me banished,
Then mightst thou speak, then mightst thou tear thy hair
And fall upon the ground as I do now,
Taking the measure of an unmade grave.   [*Knock*]   70

Friar Laurence   Arise, one knocks. Good Romeo, hide thyself.

Romeo   Not I, unless the breath of heartsick groans
Mist-like infold me from the search of eyes.   [*Knock*]

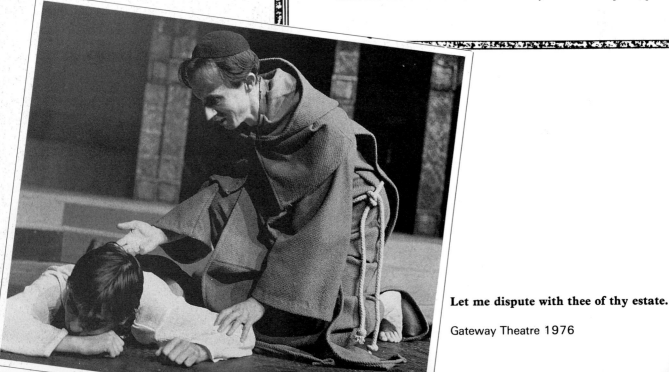

Let me dispute with thee of thy estate.

Gateway Theatre 1976

Friar Laurence   Hark how they knock! – Who's there? –
     Romeo, arise,
   Thou wilt be taken. – Stay a while! – Stand up.   *[Knock]*   **75**
   Run to my study. – By and by! – God's will,
   What simpleness is this? – I come, I come!   *[Knock]*
   Who knocks so hard? Whence come you, what's your will?

Nurse   *[Within]* Let me come in and you shall know my
     errand.
   I come from Lady Juliet.

Friar Laurence   Welcome then.   **80**

[Enter **Nurse***]*

Nurse   O holy Friar, O, tell me, holy Friar,
   Where is my lady's lord, where's Romeo?

Friar Laurence   There on the ground, with his own tears
     made drunk.

Nurse   O, he is even in my mistress' case,
   Just in her case. O woeful sympathy,   **85**
   Piteous predicament. Even so lies she,
   Blubbering and weeping, weeping and blubbering.
   Stand up, stand up. Stand, and you be a man.
   For Juliet's sake, for her sake, rise and stand.
   Why should you fall into so deep an O?   **90**

Romeo   Nurse –   *[He rises]*

Nurse   Ah sir, ah sir, death's the end of all.

Romeo   Spak'st thou of Juliet? How is it with her?
   Doth not she think me an old murderer
   Now I have stained the childhood of our joy
   With blood removed but little from her own?   **95**
   Where is she? And how doth she? And what says
   My concealed lady to our cancelled love?

Nurse   O, she says nothing, sir, but weeps and weeps,
   And now falls on her bed, and then starts up,
   And Tybalt calls, and then on Romeo cries,   **100**
   And then down falls again.

Romeo   As if that name,

---

75   **taken**   captured
     Stay awhile!   Wait a moment!
     The Friar is alternately talking to Romeo and
     shouting to whomever is at the door.
76   **By and by!**   In a moment!
77   **Simpleness**   foolishness
     To what, do you suppose, is the Friar referring?
84   **case**   state, way of behaving
85   **woeful sympathy**   mutual grief
88–90   **stand** in these lines has a bawdy double-meaning.
     Is this punning suitable at this point?
90   **O**   groan
93   **old**   hardened
97   **concealed lady**   secret wife
100   **on**   (i) for; (ii) against (Which do you think is the
     better reading?)

> Draw a sketch showing how you imagine
> the set design and where the characters are
> during the action of this page.

Doth not she think me an old murderer . . .

Bristol Old Vic 1959

102 **level** aim (an example of frequent gun imagery)
106 **sack** ransack
107 **mansion** house
108 **form** shape
110 **unreasonable** irrational
111 unbecoming womanish behaviour in one who has the appearance of a man
112 and an unnatural and inappropriate beast in appearing to be both man and woman
113 The Friar's **holy order** would have been of St Francis.
114 **disposition** character, personality
     tempered balanced (in temperament)
117 **damned** Suicide was a mortal sin and meant damnation.
118 **rail'st thou** do you complain
119- **birth . . . once** your family origins, soul and body
20   are all united in you
120 **at once** all at the same time
     wouldst lose that is, by committing suicide
121 **wit** intelligence
122 In what way do you think the Friar is comparing Romeo with a **usurer** (that is, a miserly money-lender, who uses money only to lend out at interest)?
125 **form of wax** an image which melts, and not the real thing
126 **Digressing** if it deviates
128 **killing** if it kills
130 **Misshapen** misdirected
     both that is, **shape** and **love**
131 **powder** gunpowder, which was used for firing muskets and carried in a **flask** (horn)
133 **dismembered with** blown apart by
     thine own defence that is, the intelligence which should protect you
135 **thou wast . . . dead** that is, for whom you would have killed yourself
136 **would** wanted to

Comment on Romeo's imagery in lines 106–7. (See Act II Scene 2 lines 38–51.)

Find out what you can about the old theory of the four 'humours' which were supposed to run through the body and determine each person's character.

Shot from the deadly level of a gun,
Did murder her, as that name's cursed hand
Murdered her kinsman. O, tell me, Friar, tell me,
In what vile part of this anatomy   105
Doth my name lodge? Tell me that I may sack
The hateful mansion.   [**Romeo** *draws a dagger*]

Friar Laurence   Hold thy desperate hand.
Art thou a man? Thy form cries out thou art.
Thy tears are womanish, thy wild acts denote
The unreasonable fury of a beast.   110
Unseemly woman in a seeming man,
And ill-beseeming beast in seeming both!
Thou hast amazed me. By my holy order,
I thought thy disposition better tempered.
Hast thou slain Tybalt? Wilt thou slay thyself?   115
And slay thy lady that in thy life lives,
By doing damned hate upon thyself?
Why rail'st thou on thy birth, the heaven and earth?
Since birth, and heaven, and earth all three do meet
In thee at once; which thou at once wouldst lose.   120
Fie, fie, thou sham'st thy shape, thy love, thy wit,
Which, like a usurer, abound'st in all,
And usest none in that true use indeed
Which should bedeck thy shape, thy love, thy wit.
Thy noble shape is but a form of wax   125
Digressing from the valour of a man;
Thy dear love sworn but hollow perjury,
Killing that love which thou hast vowed to cherish;
Thy wit, that ornament to shape and love,
Misshapen in the conduct of them both,   130
Like powder in a skilless soldier's flask
Is set afire by thine own ignorance,
And thou dismembered with thine own defence.
What? Rouse thee, man! Thy Juliet is alive,
For whose dear sake thou wast but lately dead.   135
There art thou happy. Tybalt would kill thee,
But thou slew'st Tybalt. There art thou happy.
The law that threatened death becomes thy friend

Redgrave Theatre 1974   **Hold thy desperate hand.**   Lyceum Theatre 1908

And turns it to exile. There art thou happy.
A pack of blessings light upon thy back; 140
Happiness courts thee in her best array;
But like a mishaved and a sullen wench
Thou pouts upon thy fortune and thy love.
Take heed, take heed, for such die miserable.
Go, get thee to thy love as was decreed, 145
Ascend her chamber – hence, and comfort her.
But look thou stay not till the Watch be set,
For then thou canst not pass to Mantua,
Where thou shalt live till we can find a time
To blaze your marriage, reconcile your friends, 150
Beg pardon of the Prince and call thee back,
With twenty hundred thousand times more joy
Than thou wentst forth in lamentation.
Go before, Nurse. Commend me to thy lady
And bid her hasten all the house to bed, 155
Which heavy sorrow makes them apt unto.
Romeo is coming.

Nurse   O lord, I could have stayed here all the night
To hear good counsel. O, what learning is.
My lord, I'll tell my lady you will come. 160

Romeo   Do so, and bid my sweet prepare to chide.

[**Nurse** *starts to go in, but turns again*]

Nurse   Here sir, a ring she bid me give you, sir.
Hie you, make haste, for it grows very late.   [*Exit*]

Romeo   How well my comfort is revived by this.

Friar Laurence   Go hence, good night, and here stands all
      your state: 165
Either be gone before the Watch be set,
Or by the break of day disguised from hence.
Sojourn in Mantua. I'll find out your man,
And he shall signify from time to time
Every good hap to you that chances here. 170
Give me thy hand. 'Tis late. Farewell. Good night.

140 **light** settle
142 **mishaved** misbehaved
143 **fortune** that is, good fortune
145 **decreed** arranged
147 **Watch** a guard posted at the gates when they
    were closed at nightfall
150 **blaze** proclaim
    friends that is, the members of both families
154 **before** ahead
156 **apt unto** ready to do
157 What is the effect of leaving unfinished this iambic
    pentameter?
161 **chide** reproach (me – for killing Tybalt)
163 **Hie** hurry
164 **comfort** happiness
165 **here ... state** your whole situation depends on
    what I am about to say
168 **Sojourn** stay
169 **signify** let (me) know
170 **hap** happening

How should Romeo react during Friar
Laurence's long sermon-like speech? How
might the actor playing Friar Laurence give
some variety in the delivery of his speech?
Note the Nurse's reaction in lines 158–9.

Provide the most suitable caption for this picture,
taken from lines 107–53 or from lines 165–71
(Act III Scene 3).

Royal Shakespeare Company 1976

173 **brief** hastily

Write down the stream of Romeo's thoughts as he makes his way from Friar Laurence's cell.

---

1 **fallen out** happened
2 **move** discuss and persuade (that she shall marry Paris)
6 **promise** assure
10 **know her mind** will find out what she thinks
11 **mewed up with her heaviness** shut up with her sorrow (falcons were kept in mews)
12 **desperate tender** bold offer
15 **ere** before
16 What detail in this line reveals Capulet's certainty in his vision of the future? Can you spot other details in this scene which suggest this?
17 **mark you me** do you note what I'm saying?
18 **soft** wait a minute
19 **Ha ha!** This is not laughter, but represents Capulet's pause for thought.
20 **A'** on
21 **earl** used here as a general term for a nobleman
23 **ado** wedding celebration
24 **late** recently
25 **carelessly** in no great esteem

Romeo   But that a joy past joy calls out on me,
It were a grief so brief to part with thee.
Farewell.   [*Exeunt*]

Scene 4

Verona. Capulet's house. Enter **Capulet**, **Lady Capulet** *and* **Paris**.

Capulet   Things have fallen out, sir, so unluckily
That we have had no time to move our daughter.
Look you, she loved her kinsman Tybalt dearly,
And so did I. Well, we were born to die.
'Tis very late. She'll not come down tonight.   5
I promise you, but for your company,
I would have been abed an hour ago.

Paris   These times of woe afford no times to woo.
Madam, good night. Commend me to your daughter.

Lady Capulet   I will, and know her mind early tomorrow.   10
Tonight she's mewed up to her heaviness.

[**Paris** *starts to go, but* **Capulet** *calls him back*]

Capulet   Sir Paris, I will make a desperate tender
Of my child's love. I think she will be ruled
In all respects by me; nay, more, I doubt it not.
Wife, go you to her ere you go to bed,   15
Acquaint her here of my son Paris' love,
And bid her – mark you me? – on Wednesday next –
But soft – what day is this?

Paris   Monday, my lord.

Capulet   Monday! Ha ha! Well, Wednesday is too soon.
A' Thursday let it be, a' Thursday, tell her,   20
She shall be married to this noble earl.
Will you be ready? Do you like this haste?
We'll keep no great ado – a friend or two.
For, hark you, Tybalt being slain so late,
It may be thought we held him carelessly,   25

Re-read lines 5–11. What hint does Capulet give to Paris, which the courteous Paris immediately acts upon? In what way are the lines ironic?
Look through for ironic details in the rest of the scene.

Things have fallen out, sir, so unluckily . . .

Albany Empire 1988

Being our kinsman, if we revel much.
Therefore we'll have some half a dozen friends
And there an end. But what say you to Thursday?

Paris   My lord, I would that Thursday were tomorrow.

Capulet   Well, get you gone. A' Thursday be it then.   30
Go you to Juliet ere you go to bed,
Prepare her, wife, against this wedding day.
Farewell, my lord. – Light to my chamber, ho!
Afore me, it is so very late that we
May call it early by and by. Good night.   35
[Exeunt]

Scene 5

The balcony outside Juliet's bedroom. Enter **Romeo** *and* **Juliet** *aloft at the window.*

Juliet   Wilt thou be gone? It is not yet near day.
It was the nightingale and not the lark
That pierced the fearful hollow of thine ear.
Nightly she sings on yond pomegranate tree.
Believe me, love, it was the nightingale.   5

Romeo   It was the lark, the herald of the morn,
No nightingale. Look, love, what envious streaks
Do lace the severing clouds in yonder east.
Night's candles are burnt out, and jocund day
Stands tiptoe on the misty mountain tops.   10
I must be gone and live, or stay and die.

Juliet   Yond light is not daylight, I know it, I.
It is some meteor that the sun exhales
To be to thee this night a torchbearer
And light thee on thy way to Mantua.   15
Therefore stay yet: thou need'st not to be gone.

Romeo   Let me be ta'en, let me be put to death;
I am content, so thou wilt have it so.
I'll say yon grey is not the morning's eye,
'Tis but the pale reflex of Cynthia's brow.   20
Nor that is not the lark whose notes do beat

27   The number of friends is growing. What does this suggest will happen? (Look ahead to Act IV Scene 4.)
32   **against**   in readiness for
34   **Afore me**   a mild oath meaning 'as God is before me' or, more simply, 'indeed'
35   **by and by**   very soon

What is the effect of the repeated **Thursday** in the second half of this scene?

---

2   **lark**   by tradition, larksong announces daybreak
3   **fearful**   It is, of course, Romeo and not his ear which is **fearful**. This is known as a 'transferred epithet', because the adjective has been 'transferred' from one noun (Romeo) to another (the hollow of his ear).
4   **yond**   yonder, the one over there
7   **envious**   malicious
8   **severing**   What else, apart from the clouds, are the streaks of light separating?
9   What do you suppose **Night's candles** to be?
     jocund   cheerful, happy
13   It was thought that meteors were caused by vapours drawn up from earth to heaven and then ignited by the sun.
17   **ta'en**   taken, captured
18   **so ... so**   if you are
20   **reflex**   reflection
     Cynthia's brow   the face of the moon (Cynthia was the goddess of the moon)
21   **Nor ... not**   Double negatives frequently appear in Shakespeare, and are a perfectly acceptable way of giving emphasis to what is being said.

**Look, love, what envious streaks
Do lace the severing clouds in yonder east.**

Royal Shakespeare Company 1976

23 **care** wish
26 **Hie** hurry
28 **sharps** shrill notes
29 **division** a series of rapid musical notes
30 **This** that is, this lark
31 **change** exchange
It was popularly believed, because the lark's eyes are ugly and the toad's beautiful, that they had exchanged eyes.
33 since that voice frightened us from each other's arms
Why does Juliet feel that the lark's voice is less fitting than the toad's as a sign for the lovers' parting?
34 **hunt's-up** (i) an early morning call to the hunt; (ii) a morning song to the newly-married bride
34-40 The Capulets must indeed have been up late (understandably so, after Tybalt's death), as Lady Capulet is carrying out her husband's insistence that she visit Juliet **ere you go to bed** (Act III Scene 4 line 15).
40 **look about** be careful
41 What do you think Juliet means by **life**?
43 **ay** forever, always
friend lover
44 **in the hour** once an hour
46 **count** reckoning
much in years old

Think about the imagery of this scene so far, particularly the images of light and darkness. Why are they used?

Hie hence, begone, away!

Temba Theatre Company 1988

The vaulty heaven so high above our heads.
I have more care to stay than will to go.
Come death, and welcome. Juliet wills it so.
How is't, my soul? Let's talk. It is not day.   25

Juliet   It is, it is. Hie hence, begone, away!
It is the lark that sings so out of tune,
Straining harsh discords and unpleasing sharps.
Some say the lark makes sweet division.
This doth not so, for she divideth us.   30
Some say the lark and loathed toad change eyes.
O, now I would they had changed voices too,
Since arm from arm that voice doth us affray,
Hunting thee hence with hunt's-up to the day.
O now be gone, more light and light it grows.   35

Romeo   More light and light: more dark and dark our woes.

[*Enter* **Nurse** *hastily*]

Nurse   Madam.

Juliet   Nurse?

Nurse   Your lady mother is coming to your chamber.
The day is broke, be wary, look about.   [*Exit*] 40

Juliet   Then, window, let day in and let life out.

Romeo   Farewell, farewell, one kiss and I'll descend.

[*He goes down the rope-ladder*]

Juliet   Art thou gone so? Love, lord, ay husband, friend,
I must hear from thee every day in the hour,
For in a minute there are many days.   45
O, by this count I shall be much in years
Ere I again behold my Romeo.

Romeo   Farewell.
I will omit no opportunity
That may convey my greetings, love, to thee.   50

Juliet   O think'st thou we shall ever meet again?

Romeo   I doubt it not, and all these woes shall serve

For sweet discourses in our times to come.

Juliet   O God, I have an ill-divining soul!
Methinks I see thee, now thou art so low,   55
As one dead in the bottom of a tomb.
Either my eyesight fails, or thou look'st pale.

Romeo   And trust me, love, in my eye so do you.
Dry sorrow drinks our blood. Adieu, adieu.

                                        [*Exit*]

Juliet   O Fortune, Fortune! All men call thee fickle;   60
If thou art fickle, what dost thou with him
That is renowned for faith? Be fickle, Fortune,
For then I hope thou wilt not keep him long,
But send him back.

[*Enter* **Lady Capulet**]

Lady Capulet   Ho, daughter, are you up?

Juliet   [*Aside*] Who is't that calls? It is my lady mother.   65
Is she not down so late, or up so early?
What unaccustomed cause procures her hither?

                        [*She withdraws from the window*]

Lady Capulet   Why, how now Juliet?

[*Enter* **Juliet**]

Juliet   Madam, I am not well.

Lady Capulet   Evermore weeping for your cousin's death?
What, wilt thou wash him from his grave with tears?   70
And if thou couldst, thou couldst not make him live.
Therefore have done: some grief shows much of love,
But much of grief shows still some want of wit.

Juliet   Yet let me weep for such a feeling loss.

Lady Capulet   So shall you feel the loss but not the friend   75
Which you weep for.

---

53 **sweet discourses** pleasant conversation
54 **ill-divining** anticipating evil
55 **now thou art so low** In view of these words, where do you think Romeo and Juliet are placed on stage in relation to each other?
59 **Dry** thirsty
      It was supposed that sorrow drank the body's blood, so making the face pale.
60 **fickle** unreliable
61 **dost thou** are you doing
62 **faith** steadfastness
66 **down** going to bed
67 **procures** draws
68 **how now . . . ?** what's the matter . . . ?
72 **shows** is evidence of
73 **much of** too much display of
      still always
      wit intelligence
74 **feeling** deeply felt
75-6 **but not . . . for** that is, because Tybalt cannot come alive again

---

Comment on the ironies of lines 69–77.

In lines 72–3, do you think Lady Capulet is talking about real sorrow, or about the display of that sorrow?

The setting of the scene begins outside Juliet's bedroom, but continues inside it. How would you set this scene. Draw a diagram to illustrate it.

**Methinks I see thee, now thou art so low,
As one dead in the bottom of a tomb.**

Royal Shakespeare Company 1989

77   **choose** help
      weep weep for
      friend apparently meaning Tybalt, but see note to
      line 43 of this scene
81   That is, the word 'villain' and 'Romeo' do not go
      together.
83   **like** as much as
88   **Mantua** Lady Capulet cannot yet know of
      Romeo's destination; and he cannot yet have
      arrived there, having only just left Juliet. Do you
      think this kind of carelessness on Shakespeare's
      part is important?
89   **runagate** outlaw
90   **unaccustomed dram** unusual dose (of poison)
94   **dead** Juliet is referring ahead to **my poor heart**,
      but ambiguously allows her mother to think that she
      is referring back to *Romeo*. Likewise **kinsman** in
      line 95 could refer to Tybalt or to Romeo.
97   **temper** (i) mix; (ii) make more moderate
101   **wreak** (i) avenge; (ii) display
105   **needy** that is, in need of happiness
107   **careful** full of care (for your good)
108   **heaviness** unhappiness
109   **sudden** unexpected

Look closely at all the double-meanings which Juliet uses (and which her mother cannot appreciate).

But now I'll tell thee joyful tidings, girl.

Royal Shakespeare Company 1976

Juliet   Feeling so the loss,
      I cannot choose but ever weep the friend.

Lady Capulet   Well, girl, thou weepst not so much for his death
      As that the villain lives which slaughtered him.

Juliet   What villain, madam?

Lady Capulet   That same villain Romeo.   80

Juliet   [*Aside*] Villain and he be many miles asunder.
      [*Aloud*] God pardon him. I do with all my heart.
      And yet no man like he doth grieve my heart.

Lady Capulet   That is because the traitor murderer lives.

Juliet   Ay madam, from the reach of these my hands.   85
      Would none but I might venge my cousin's death.

Lady Capulet   We will have vengeance for it, fear thou not.
      Then weep no more. I'll send to one in Mantua,
      Where that same banished runagate doth live,
      Shall give him such an unaccustomed dram   90
      That he shall soon keep Tybalt company;
      And then I hope thou wilt be satisfied.

Juliet   Indeed I never shall be satisfied
      With Romeo, till I behold him – dead –
      Is my poor heart so for a kinsman vexed.   95
      Madam, if you could find out but a man
      To bear a poison, I would temper it –
      That Romeo should upon receipt thereof
      Soon sleep in quiet. O, how my heart abhors
      To hear him named, and cannot come to him   100
      To wreak the love I bore my cousin
      Upon his body that hath slaughtered him.

Lady Capulet   Find thou the means and I'll find such a man.
      But now I'll tell thee joyful tidings, girl.

Juliet   And joy comes well in such a needy time.   105
      What are they, I beseech your ladyship?

Lady Capulet   Well, well, thou hast a careful father, child;
      One who to put thee from thy heaviness
      Hath sorted out a sudden day of joy,

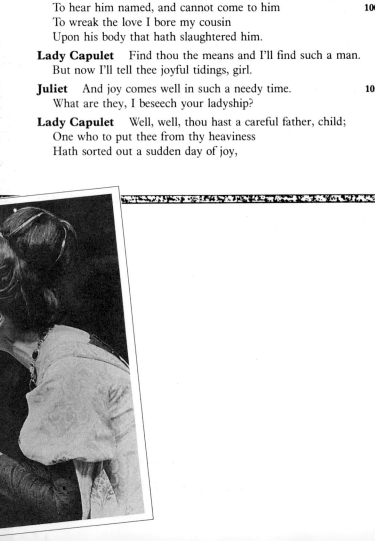

That thou expects not, nor I looked not for.   110

Juliet   Madam, in happy time. What day is that?

Lady Capulet   Marry, my child, early next Thursday morn
The gallant, young, and noble gentleman,
The County Paris, at Saint Peter's Church,
Shall happily make thee there a joyful bride.   115

Juliet   Now by Saint Peter's Church, and Peter too,
He shall not make me there a joyful bride.
I wonder at this haste, that I must wed
Ere he that should be husband comes to woo.
I pray you tell my lord and father, madam,   120
I will not marry yet. And when I do, I swear
It shall be Romeo, whom you know I hate,
Rather than Paris. These are news indeed.

Lady Capulet   Here comes your father, tell him so yourself,
And see how he will take it at your hands.   125

[*Enter* **Capulet** *and* **Nurse**]

Capulet   When the sun sets the earth doth drizzle dew,
But for the sunset of my brother's son
It rains downright.
How now, a conduit, girl? What, still in tears?
Evermore showering? In one little body   130
Thou counterfeits a bark, a sea, a wind.
For still thy eyes, which I may call the sea,
Do ebb and flow with tears. The bark thy body is,
Sailing in this salt flood, the winds thy sighs,
Who raging with thy tears and they with them,   135
Without a sudden calm will overset
Thy tempest-tossed body. How now, wife?
Have you delivered to her our decree?

Lady Capulet   Ay sir, but she will none, she gives you thanks.
I would the fool were married to her grave.   140

Capulet   Soft, take me with you, take me with you, wife.
How? Will she none? Doth she not give us thanks?
Is she not proud? Doth she not count her blest,

110 nor...for Far from cancelling out each other, double negatives add emphasis.
111 in happy time this is fortunate at this time
114 County Count
119 should expects to be
126-8 Capulet means that Juliet is crying at the setting of Tybalt's sun (that is, his death).
129 conduit fountain
Water spouts often came from a human figure. What effect do you think this gives to Capulet's words to Juliet?
131 counterfeits are like
bark boat
136 overset overturn
138 What does the tone of this line tell you about Capulet's attitude towards his family? (See also lines 141 and following.)
139 none have nothing to do with it
141 Soft go slowly, just a minute
take me with you let me understand you
143 proud pleased
count her consider herself

What, still in tears?

Royal Shakespeare Company 1976

144 wrought arranged
145 bride used for either sex in Shakespeare's time
146 you have that you have
    thankful that you have that is, that you have
    been so thoughtful of me
148 love lovingly
149 chopped logic mixed logic, illogical argument
151 minion young minx, spoilt child
152 proud Shakespeare often changed adjectives and
    nouns into verbs.
153 fettle groom a horse, but here used generally to
    mean 'get ready'
155 hurdle flat frame to which traitors were tied and
    hauled through the streets to the place of their
    execution.
156–7 green-sickness carrion . . . tallow face referring
    to the sickly paleness of Juliet's face
    (**tallow** = candle-wax)
157 Who do you think Lady Capulet is addressing –
    Juliet or her husband?
161 a' on
164 In what sense do you think Capulet's fingers **itch**?
168 hilding inferior horse, useless creature
169 rate berate, scold
171 Smatter chatter
172 God-i-good e'en Good evening! (spoken
    sarcastically)

Gateway Theatre 1976

Unworthy as she is, that we have wrought
So worthy a gentleman to be her bride?   **145**

Juliet   Not proud you have, but thankful that you have.
Proud can I never be of what I hate,
But thankful even for hate that is meant love.

Capulet   How, how, how, how? Chopped logic? What is this?
'Proud' and 'I thank you' and 'I thank you not'   **150**
And yet 'not proud'? Mistress minion you,
Thank me no thankings, nor proud me no prouds,
But fettle your fine joints 'gainst Thursday next
To go with Paris to Saint Peter's Church,
Or I will drag thee on a hurdle thither.   **155**
Out, you green-sickness carrion! Out, you baggage!
You tallow-face!

Lady Capulet   Fie, fie. What, are you mad?

Juliet   Good father, I beseech you on my knees,
Hear me with patience but to speak a word.

                                     [She kneels down]

Capulet   Hang thee young baggage, disobedient wretch!   **160**
I tell thee what – get thee to church a' Thursday
Or never after look me in the face.
Speak not, reply not, do not answer me.
My fingers itch. Wife, we scarce thought us blest
That God had lent us but this only child;   **165**
But now I see this one is one too much,
And that we have a curse in having her.
Out on her, hilding.

Nurse   God in heaven bless her.
You are to blame, my lord, to rate her so.

Capulet   And why, my Lady Wisdom? Hold your tongue,   **170**
Good Prudence! Smatter with your gossips, go.

Nurse   I speak no treason.

Capulet   O God-i-good e'en!

Nurse   May not one speak?

You tallow-face!

Bristol Old Vic 1966

Capulet   Peace, you mumbling fool!
Utter your gravity o'er a gossip's bowl,
For here we need it not.

Lady Capulet   You are too hot.   175

Capulet   God's bread, it makes me mad! Day, night, work, play,
Alone, in company, still my care hath been
To have her matched. And having now provided
A gentleman of noble parentage,
Of fair demesnes, youthful and nobly ligned,   180
Stuffed, as they say, with honourable parts,
Proportioned as one's thought would wish a man –
And then to have a wretched puling fool,
A whining mammet, in her fortune's tender,
To answer 'I'll not wed, I cannot love,   185
I am too young, I pray you pardon me!'
But, and you will not wed, I'll pardon you!
Graze where you will, you shall not house with me.
Look to't, think on't, I do not use to jest.
Thursday is near. Lay hand on heart. Advise.   190
And you be mine I'll give you to my friend;
And you be not, hang! Beg! Starve! Die in the streets!
For by my soul I'll ne'er acknowledge thee,
Nor what is mine shall never do thee good.
Trust to't, bethink you. I'll not be forsworn.   [*Exit*]   195

Juliet   Is there no pity sitting in the clouds
That sees into the bottom of my grief?
O sweet my mother, cast me not away,
Delay this marriage for a month, a week,
Or if you do not, make the bridal bed   200
In that dim monument where Tybalt lies.

Lady Capulet   Talk not to me, for I'll not speak a word.
Do as thou wilt, for I have done with thee.   [*Exit*]

Juliet   O God, O Nurse, how shall this be prevented?
My husband is on earth, my faith in heaven.   205
How shall that faith return again to earth
Unless that husband send it me from heaven
By leaving earth? Comfort me, counsel me.

174 **gravity** wisdom (again, sarcastic)
     gossip's bowl when socialising with your gossips
175 **hot** angry
176 **God's bread** by the consecrated bread of the
     Communion service
     How strong an oath do you think this is?
176– Capulet is trying to present the image of himself as
82   a caring father. How caring do you find him in the
     play as a whole?
178 **matched** married
180 **demesnes** estates, property
     ligned descended (that is, of a good family)
181 **parts** qualities
183 **puling** snivelling
184 **mammet** puppet, doll
     in . . . tender when good fortune is offered
187 **and** if
     I'll pardon you! In what sense do you think
     Capulet will **pardon** Juliet (in a way that she will
     not like)?
188 **house** See note to line 152.
189 **use to** usually
190 **Advise** consider carefully
191 **mine** Capulet's attitude is quite usual for fathers at
     this time.
195 **bethink you** think about it
     be foresworn break my oath (to Paris)
     What does this reveal of Capulet's priorities?
200-1 an ironic anticipation of Act V Scene 5
205 **faith** register of my marriage vows
207-8 **Unless . . . earth** that is, unless Romeo dies

Write or improvise an argument between a parent and a son or daughter. Try not to show all the sympathy with one side.

Re-read lines 126–95. Then look back and re-read Act I Scene 2 lines 1–37 and Act I Scene 5 lines 14–89. Now consider how widely Capulet's attitude and behaviour vary on these three occasions. To what extent, do you think, is Capulet responsible for bringing about the death of his daughter?

Albany Empire 1988

209 **stratagems** tricks
213 **all . . . nothing** the odds are infinite
214 **challenge** claim (as his wife)
219 **dishclout** dishcloth compared to
220 **green** green eyes were considered rare and to be admired
    quick keen (eagles were renowned for the keenness of their eyesight)
222 **Beshrew** cursed be
224 **'t** it
225 **living** that is, you (Juliet) living here
    use The Nurse talks of Romeo as if he is merely a sex object.
227 **them both** that is, both my heart and soul
228 **Amen!** So be it!
229 **What?** Does the Nurse understand that Juliet is saying 'Amen!' to the Nurse's curse on herself? Or does she think that Juliet is agreeing to the suggestion that she should forget Romeo and marry Paris?
235 **Ancient damnation!** Cursed old woman!
236 **sin** sinful
    forsworn to break my (marriage) vows
238 **with above compare** as being beyond comparison
240 **twain** separated
    Juliet means that she will never again take the Nurse into her confidence.

Shakespeare is often careless about the passage of time, possibly because the exact passing of time does not much matter. However, construct your own timetable for the events of Act III.

Speakest thou from thy heart?

Royal Shakespeare Company 1983

Alack, alack, that heaven should practise stratagems
Upon so soft a subject as myself.   210
What sayst thou? Hast thou not a word of joy?
Some comfort, Nurse.

Nurse   Faith, here it is.
Romeo is banished, and all the world to nothing
That he dares ne'er come back to challenge you.
Or if he do, it needs must be by stealth.   215
Then, since the case so stands as now it doth,
I think it best you married with the County.
O, he's a lovely gentleman.
Romeo's a dishclout to him. An eagle, madam,
Hath not so green, so quick, so fair an eye   220
As Paris hath. Beshrew my very heart,
I think you are happy in this second match,
For it excels your first; or, if it did not,
Your first is dead, or 'twere as good he were
As living here and you no use of him.   225

Juliet Speakest thou from thy heart?

Nurse And from my soul too, else beshrew them both.

Juliet Amen.

Nurse What?

Juliet Well, thou hast comforted me marvellous much. 230
Go in, and tell my lady I am gone,
Having displeased my father, to Laurence' cell,
To make confession and to be absolved.

Nurse Marry, I will; and this is wisely done.   [*Exit*]

Juliet Ancient damnation! O most wicked fiend,   235
Is it more sin to wish me thus forsworn,
Or to dispraise my lord with that same tongue
Which she hath praised him with above compare
So many thousand times? Go, counsellor.
Thou and my bosom henceforth shall be twain.   240
I'll to the Friar to know his remedy.
If all else fail, myself have power to die.

[*Exit*]

Act IV

Scene 1

*Friar Laurence's cell. Enter **Friar Laurence** and **Paris**.*

Friar Laurence   On Thursday, sir? The time is very short.

Paris   My father Capulet will have it so,
And I am nothing slow to slack his haste.

Friar Laurence   You say you do not know the lady's mind.
Uneven is the course. I like it not.   5

Paris   Immoderately she weeps for Tybalt's death,
And therefore have I little talked of love,
For Venus smiles not in a house of tears.
Now sir, her father counts it dangerous
That she do give her sorrow so much sway,   10
And in his wisdom hastes our marriage
To stop the inundation of her tears
Which, too much minded by herself alone,
May be put from her by society.
Now do you know the reason of this haste.   15

Friar Laurence   [*Aside*] I would I knew not why it should be
        slowed –
    [*Aloud*] Look sir, here comes the lady toward my cell.

[*Enter **Juliet***]

Paris   Happily met, my lady and my wife.

Juliet   That may be, sir, when I may be a wife.

Paris   That may be, must be, love, on Thursday next.   20

Juliet   What must be, shall be.

Friar Laurence   That's a certain text.

Paris   Come you to make confession to this father?

Juliet   To answer that, I should confess to you.

2 **father**   that is, prospective father-in-law
3 **nothing slow**   by no means reluctant
5 **Uneven**   unsatisfactory, one-sided
8 In this line there are secondary astrological allusions
   to the planet Venus and to the twelve parts or
   'houses' into which the heavens are divided. But
   what do you think is the main meaning of this line?
9 **counts**   accounts, considers
13 that is, when she is alone she is too easily able to
    think about the reason for her tears
14 **society**   the company of others
15 **do you**   a statement, not a question

Zeffirelli 1968

26 **will ye** you will (confess to the Friar)
27 **price** value, worth
32 **it** that is, your face
34 **to my face** (i) openly; (ii) about my face
35 What do you think Paris means by this?
36 In what way is Juliet's reply ironic?
39 **pensive** sad
40 **entreat...alone** beg to be left together in private
41 **shield** forbid
47 What statement do you think Friar Laurence is making about his ability to think about the problem? Draw a sketch to illustrate the compass image.
48 **prorogue** postpone
53 What has Juliet resolved to do if the Friar approves of her **resolution**?
54 **knife** small knives were often carried at the girdle by Elizabethan ladies
   presently immediately
56 **ere** before
56-7 Juliet uses legal imagery with **sealed** (contracted), **label** (a codicil or addendum to a contract) and **deed** (contract).

Consider lines 18–43. Is there any change in the style of the verse when Juliet enters and talks with Paris? If so, why? What is Juliet's tone towards Paris? Is she changing as a person?

Paris   Do not deny to him that you love me.

Juliet   I will confess to you that I love him.   25

Paris   So will ye, I am sure, that you love me.

Juliet   If I do so, it will be of more price
Being spoke behind your back than to your face.

Paris   Poor soul, thy face is much abused with tears.

Juliet   The tears have got small victory by that,   30
For it was bad enough before their spite.

Paris   Thou wrong'st it more than tears with that report.

Juliet   That is no slander, sir, which is a truth,
And what I spake, I spake it to my face.

Paris   Thy face is mine, and thou hast slandered it.   35

Juliet   It may be so, for it is not mine own. –
Are you at leisure, holy father, now,
Or shall I come to you at evening mass?

Friar Laurence   My leisure serves me, pensive daughter, now. –
My lord, we must entreat the time alone.   40

Paris   God shield I should disturb devotion.
Juliet, on Thursday early will I rouse ye;
Till then, adieu, and keep this holy kiss.

[*He kisses her, then exits*]

Juliet   O shut the door, and when thou hast done so,
Come weep with me, past hope, past cure, past help!   45

Friar Laurence   O Juliet, I already know thy grief;
It strains me past the compass of my wits.
I hear thou must – and nothing may prorogue it –
On Thursday next be married to this County.

Juliet   Tell me not, Friar, that thou hearest of this,   50
Unless thou tell me how I may prevent it.
If in thy wisdom thou canst give no help,
Do thou but call my resolution wise,
And with this knife I'll help it presently
God joined my heart and Romeo's, thou our hands;   55
And ere this hand, by thee to Romeo's sealed,

O Juliet, I already know thy grief

Redgrave Theatre 1974

Shall be the label to another deed,
Or my true heart with treacherous revolt
Turn to another, this shall slay them both.
Therefore, out of thy long-experienced time   60
Give me some present counsel, or behold,
'Twixt my extremes and me this bloody knife
Shall play the umpire, arbitrating that
Which the commission of thy years and art
Could to no issue of true honour bring.   65
Be not so long to speak. I long to die
If what thou speakest speak not of remedy.

Friar Laurence   Hold, daughter. I do spy a kind of hope
Which craves as desperate an execution
As that is desperate which we would prevent.   70
If, rather than to marry County Paris,
Thou hast the strength of will to slay thyself,
Then is it likely thou wilt undertake
A thing like death to chide away this shame,
That cop'st with death himself to scape from it.   75
And if thou dar'st, I'll give thee remedy.

Juliet   O, bid me leap, rather than marry Paris,
From off the battlements of any tower,
Or walk in thievish ways, or bid me lurk
Where serpents are. Chain me with roaring bears,   80
Or hide me nightly in a charnel-house
O'ercovered quite with dead men's rattling bones,
With reeky shanks and yellow chapless skulls.
Or bid me go into a new-made grave,
And hide me with a dead man in his shroud –   85
Things that, to hear them told, have made me tremble –
And I will do it without fear or doubt,
To live an unstained wife to my sweet love.

Friar Laurence   Hold then. Go home, be merry, give consent
To marry Paris. Wednesday is tomorrow;   90
Tomorrow night look that thou lie alone.
Let not the Nurse lie with thee in thy chamber.
Take thou this vial, being then in bed,

59 **this** that is, this knife
   both that is, both hand and heart
60 **thy long-experienced time** the wisdom of your age
61 **present** immediate
62 **extremes** extreme difficulties
64 **commission** authority
   art skill
66 **Be not so long** do not be so slow
70 **that** that thing
75 **That cop'st** who is willing to face death
   it that is, death
79 **thievish ways** paths where thieves are common
81 **charnel-house** a small building attached to a church, where the bones and skulls which had been unearthed during the digging of new graves were placed
83 **reeky** foul-smelling
   chapless with lower jaw missing
89 **Hold** wait, enough
91 **look** ensure

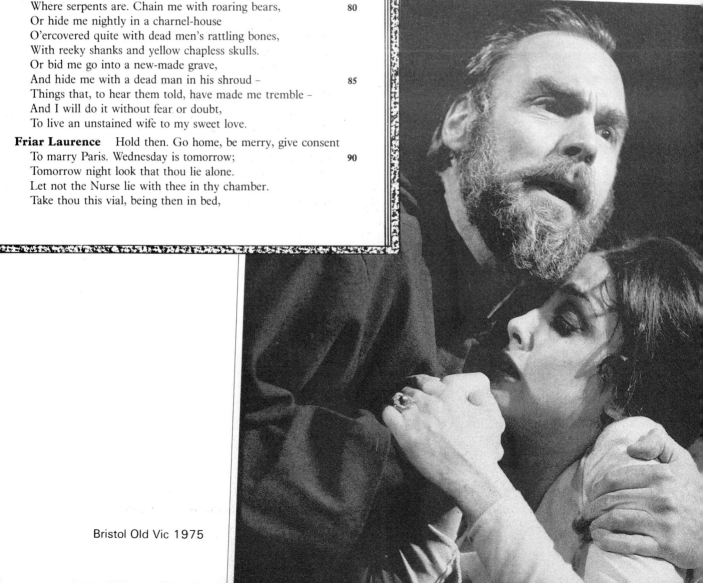

Bristol Old Vic 1975

94 **distilling** either 'distilled' or 'infusing through the body'
96 **A cold ... fluid** a liquid which induces a cold and drowsy feeling
97 **native** natural
surcease stop
100 **wanny** pale
eyes' windows eyelids
102 **supple government** control over movement
103 **stark** rigid
113 **against** in readiness for the time when
114 **drift** plan, intention
119 **inconstant toy** trifling consideration which makes you waver from your firm resolution
Note Juliet's response to this and the following line.
125 **afford** offer

**Then as the manner of our country is,
In thy best robes ...**

Young Vic 1987–8

And this distilling liquor drink thou off;
When presently through all thy veins shall run   95
A cold and drowsy humour, for no pulse
Shall keep his native progress, but surcease:
No warmth, no breath shall testify thou livest;
The roses in thy lips and cheeks shall fade
To wanny ashes, thy eyes' windows fall   100
Like death when he shuts up the day of life.
Each part deprived of supple government
Shall stiff and stark and cold appear, like death,
And in this borrowed likeness of shrunk death
Thou shalt continue two and forty hours   105
And then awake as from a pleasant sleep.
Now when the bridegroom in the morning comes
To rouse thee from thy bed, there art thou, dead.
Then as the manner of our country is,
In thy best robes, uncovered on the bier   110
Thou shall be borne to that same ancient vault
Where all the kindred of the Capulets lie.
In the meantime, against thou shalt awake,
Shall Romeo by my letters know our drift
And hither shall he come, and he and I   115
Will watch thy waking, and that very night
Shall Romeo bear thee hence to Mantua,
And this shall free thee from this present shame,
If no inconstant toy nor womanish fear
Abate thy valour in the acting it.   120

Juliet Give me, give me! O tell not me of fear.

Friar Laurence Hold. Get you gone. Be strong and prosperous
In this resolve. I'll send a friar with speed
To Mantua with my letters to thy lord.

Juliet Love give me strength, and strength shall help afford. 125
Farewell, dear father.   [*Exeunt*]

Scene 2

Verona. Capulet's house. Enter **Capulet**, **Lady Capulet**, **Nurse**
and two or three **Servants**.

Capulet   So many guests invite as here are writ.

                                  [Exit **Servant***]*

    Sirrah, go hire me twenty cunning cooks.

Servant   You shall have none ill, for I'll try if they can lick
their fingers.

Capulet   How! Canst thou try them so?   5

Servant   Marry sir, 'tis an ill cook that cannot lick his own
fingers; therefore he that cannot lick his fingers goes not with
me.

Capulet   Go, be gone.   *[Exit* **Servant***]*
We shall be much unfurnished for this time.   10
What, is my daughter gone to Friar Laurence?

Nurse   Ay, forsooth.

Capulet   Well, he may chance to do some good on her.
A peevish self-willed harlotry it is.

[Enter **Juliet***]*

Nurse   See where she comes from shrift with merry look.   15

Capulet   How now, my headstrong: where have you been
        gadding?

Juliet   Where I have learnt me to repent the sin
Of disobedient opposition
To you and your behests, and am enjoined
By holy Laurence to fall prostrate here,   20
To beg your pardon. Pardon, I beseech you.
Henceforward I am ever ruled by you.

                              [She kneels down]

Capulet   Send for the County, go tell him of this.
I'll have this knot knit up tomorrow morning.

2   **cunning**   skilled, expert
In hiring so many cooks, has Capulet forgotten what
he said to Paris in Act III Scene 4? What may this
show about Capulet's character?

3   **none ill**   no bad ones
try   test
There was a proverb which said that only a poor
cook would not want to lick his own fingers to taste
the food he was preparing.

10   **unfurnished**   unprepared
Yet, despite what he says here and Lady Capulet's
protests (line 36), within a minute Capulet has
brought the wedding forward to Wednesday (line
24). This impulsive change will prove fatal.

12   **forsooth**   in truth, indeed

14   **harlotry**   hussy

15   **shrift**   confession

16   What do you think is the tone of this line? How
should the actor playing Capulet deliver it?

19   **behests**   commands
enjoined   instructed

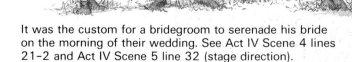

It was the custom for a bridegroom to serenade his bride
on the morning of their wedding. See Act IV Scene 4 lines
21–2 and Act IV Scene 5 line 32 (stage direction).

26 becomèd becoming, befitting, seemly
Why is there an accent over the second 'e' of
'becomèd'?
28 on't of it
29 as't as it
32 bound indebted
33 closet private room
34 sort choose
35 to furnish me for me to wear
38 provision How many syllables do you think were
pronounced in this word (note the metre)? What
'provision' do you suppose Lady Capulet is thinking
of?
39 stir about get to work on it
40 warrant guarantee, assure
41 deck up decorate (in the sense of dress and put
adornments or jewellery on)
42 let me alone leave me to it
44 They are all forth the servants are all out of the
house on errands
46 Against in readiness for

1 attires clothes
2 In what way is Juliet following the Friar's
instructions?
3 orisons prayers
4 state condition, situation
5 cross unfavourable, perverse
In what tone of voice do you think Juliet should talk
to the Nurse here?

Juliet   I met the youthful lord at Laurence' cell,   25
And gave him what becomèd love I might,
Not stepping o'er the bounds of modesty.

Capulet   Why, I am glad on't. This is well. Stand up.
This is as't should be. Let me see the County.
Ay, marry. Go, I say, and fetch him hither.   30
Now afore God, this reverend holy Friar,
All our whole city is much bound to him.

Juliet   Nurse, will you go with me into my closet,
To help me sort such needful ornaments
As you think fit to furnish me tomorrow?   35

Lady Capulet   No, not till Thursday. There is time enough.

Capulet   Go, Nurse, go with her. We'll to church tomorrow.
                                        [*Exeunt* **Juliet** *and* **Nurse**]

Lady Capulet   We shall be short in our provision,
'Tis now near night.

Capulet   Tush, I will stir about,
And all things shall be well, I warrant thee, wife.   40
Go thou to Juliet, help to deck up her.
I'll not to bed tonight, let me alone.
I'll play the housewife for this once. [*He calls for servants*]
    What ho!
They are all forth. Well, I will walk myself
To County Paris, to prepare up him   45
Against tomorrow. My heart is wondrous light
Since this same wayward girl is so reclaimed.
                                        [*Exeunt*]

Scene 3

Verona. Capulet's house. Enter **Juliet** *and* **Nurse**.

Juliet   Ay, those attires are best. But, gentle Nurse,
I pray thee leave me to myself tonight,
For I have need of many orisons
To move the heavens to smile upon my state,
Which, well thou know'st, is cross and full of sin.   5

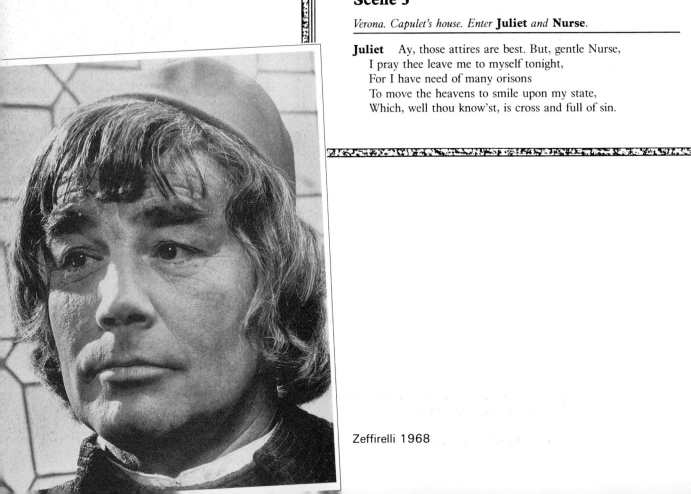

Zeffirelli 1968

[*Enter* **Lady Capulet**]

Lady Capulet   What, are you busy, ho? Need you my help?

Juliet   No madam, we have culled such necessaries
As are behoveful for our state tomorrow.
So please you, let me now be left alone
And let the Nurse this night sit up with you,   10
For I am sure you have your hands full all
In this so sudden business.

Lady Capulet   Good night.
Get thee to bed and rest, for thou hast need.

                    [*Exeunt* **Lady Capulet** *and* **Nurse**]

Juliet   Farewell. God knows when we shall meet again.
I have a faint cold fear thrills through my veins   15
That almost freezes up the heat of life.
I'll call them back again to comfort me.
– Nurse! – What should she do here?
My dismal scene I needs must act alone.
Come, vial.   20
What if this mixture do not work at all?
Shall I be married then tomorrow morning?
No! No! This shall forbid it. Lie thou there.

                    [*She lays down a knife*]

What if it be a poison which the Friar
Subtly hath ministered to have me dead,   25
Lest in this marriage he should be dishonoured,
Because he married me before to Romeo?
I fear it is. And yet methinks it should not,
For he hath still been tried a holy man.
How if, when I am laid into the tomb,   30
I wake before the time that Romeo
Come to redeem me? There's a fearful point!
Shall I not then be stifled in the vault,
To whose foul mouth no healthsome air breathes in,
And there die strangled ere my Romeo comes?   35
Or, if I live, is it not very like,
The horrible conceit of death and night
Together with the terror of the place,

7   **culled**   selected
8   **behoveful**   fitting
    In lines 7–8 what secondary meaning, unknown to
    her mother, could Juliet have in her mind?
    state   (i) social status; (ii) state of marriage;
    (iii) situation
12   How many syllables would you say 'business' has
    here? (Note the rhythm of the line.)
15   **faint cold fear**   fear which causes a chill faintness
20   What is the effect of leaving this line brief and
    incomplete?
24–8   Is Juliet's fear a reasonable one?
25   **Subtly**   cunningly
    ministered   supplied
29   **still been tried**   always proved to be
32   **redeem**   reclaim
35   **strangled**   suffocated
    ere   before
36   **like**   likely
37   **conceit**   thought, imaginings, fantasies

My dismal scene I needs must act alone.
What is the dramatic effect of isolating Juliet
towards the end of the play?

WAGEMAN DEL.   T. WOOLNOTH. SC.
MISS F. H. KELLY AS JULIET.
PUBLISHED, WEDNESDAY, APRIL 1823, BY J. DOLBY, 299. STRAND

**Shall I be married then tomorrow morning?
No! No! This shall forbid it.**

Theatre Royal, Covent Garden 1822

39 As as being
42 Yet . . . earth freshly buried
Why does she call him **bloody**?
45 like likely
46 So early waking Why is it that Juliet will wake up a long time before Romeo comes? See the previous scene.
47 mandrakes It was supposed that the mandrake plant, when pulled from the ground, shrieked – so that anyone who heard it went mad or died.
48 That so that
50 Environed This verb is not in common use today, but you should be able to work out its meaning from words of similar form which are frequently used.
53 rage madness, frenzy
great that is, of a previous generation (as in 'great grandfather')
The word does not mean 'important' here.
54 desperate brains It is not literally her brains, but she herself, who is desperate. This figure of speech is known as a 'transferred epithet', because the epithet (the adjective) has been transferred from the person to the thing. However, the effectiveness of this device is that the meaning is made quite clear.
56 spit fix as on a spit
57 Stay stop
58 Some editors prefer the reading from the second quarto (contemporary printed edition), which goes **Romeo, I come! This do I drink for thee**, because this line better fits the metre. However, the line as given here (from the first quarto), while not fitting the metre, shows expressively Juliet's mounting hysteria and loss of control. Which do you prefer?

Re-read lines 14 to the end of Scene 3. Consider (a) presentation of character, (b) dramatic interest and (c) poetic qualities.

SD It is clear that the next scene must flow on directly, but it is unclear whether Shakespeare intended Juliet to be on a four-poster bed which is specially brought on, and within whose curtains she falls; or whether she falls backwards on to a bed on the inner stage. In view of the events of the following scene, which staging would you have preferred had you been working in the Elizabethan theatre?
2 pastry the area of the kitchen where the pastry was made
3 stir get going!
second cock According to convention, cockerels crowed for the second time at 3.00am, the first crowing being at midnight and the third and final one an hour before daybreak.
4 curfew bell originally used in the evenings as a warning to people to cover their fires, but also rung at other times to signify the time

---

As in a vault, an ancient receptacle
Where for this many hundred years the bones   40
Of all my buried ancestors are packed,
Where bloody Tybalt yet but green in earth
Lies festering in his shroud; where, as they say,
At some hours in the night spirits resort –
Alack, alack! Is it not like that I   45
So early waking, what with loathsome smells,
And shrieks like mandrakes torn out of the earth,
That living mortals, hearing them, run mad –
O, if I wake, shall I not be distraught,
Environed with all these hideous fears,   50
And madly play with my forefathers' joints,
And pluck the mangled Tybalt from his shroud,
And, in this rage, with some great kinsman's bone
As with a club dash out my desperate brains?
O look, methinks I see my cousin's ghost   55
Seeking out Romeo that did spit his body
Upon a rapier's point! Stay, Tybalt, stay!
Romeo, Romeo, Romeo, here's drink! I drink to thee!
                    [*She falls upon her bed within the curtains*]

Scene 4

The same. Enter **Lady Capulet** *and* **Nurse**.

Lady Capulet   Hold, take these keys and fetch more spices,
    Nurse.

Nurse   They call for dates and quinces in the pastry.

[*Enter* **Capulet**]

Capulet   Come, stir, stir, stir, the second cock hath crowed!
    The curfew bell hath rung, 'tis three o'clock.

I drink to thee!

Royal Shakespeare Company 1976

Look to the baked meats, good Angelica: 5
Spare not for cost.

Nurse   Go, you cot-quean, go,
Get you to bed. Faith, you'll be sick tomorrow
For this night's watching.

Capulet   No, not a whit. What, I have watched ere now
All night for lesser cause, and ne'er been sick. 10

Lady Capulet   Ay, you have been a mouse-hunt in your time;
But I will watch you from such watching now.
                    [*Exeunt* **Lady Capulet** *and* **Nurse**]

Capulet   A jealous hood, a jealous hood!

[*Enter three or four* **Servants** *with spits and logs and baskets*]

                         Now fellow, what is there?

1st Servant   Things for the cook, sir, but I know not what.

Capulet   Make haste, make haste!   [*Exit* **1st Servant**]
                    – Sirrah, fetch drier logs! 15
Call Peter, he will show thee where they are.

2nd Servant   I have a head, sir, that will find out logs
And never trouble Peter for the matter.

Capulet   Mass and well said! A merry whoreson, ha.
Thou shalt be loggerhead!   [*Exit* **2nd Servant**]
                    – Good faith! 'Tis day! 20
                         [*Play music*]

The County will be here with music straight,
For so he said he would. I hear him near.
Nurse! Wife! What ho! What, Nurse I say!

[*Enter* **Nurse**]

Go waken Juliet, go, and trim her up.
I'll go and chat with Paris. Hie, make haste, 25
Make haste! The bridegroom he is come already.
Make haste I say.

                         [*Exeunt* **Capulet** *and* **Servants**]

5 **baked meats**   meat pies
   Angelica   possibly Lady Capulet, but probably the
   Nurse, since she answers; if the latter, there is a
   nice comic irony as Angelica was the beautiful
   pagan princess who cruelly flirted with many
   princes in *Orlando Furioso* (1516) by Ariosto
   (1474–1533). This work was very popular and
   Shakespeare must have read it.

6–8 Some editors think that this speech is mistakenly
   ascribed to the Nurse because she would not dare
   to speak thus to her master. What do you think?

6 **cot-quean**   a man who interferes in household
   matters

8 **watching**   staying awake

9 **not a whit**   not at all

11 **mouse-hunt**   woman-chaser
   What is Capulet hinting at in the previous two lines,
   which Lady Capulet here picks up? Is she amused
   or scornful?

12 **watch you from**   keep an eye on so that you stop

13 **hood**   that is, woman
   Can you think how the word comes to be used thus
   (consider the phrases 'big wig' or 'bad hat')?

17 The servant means that he has common sense in
   his head to find logs; but Capulet cannot resist
   picking up a punning meaning of 'blockhead'
   (**loggerhead**) in line 20.

19 **Mass**   by the mass
   whoreson   fellow (literally, son of a whore; and,
   therefore, bastard)

21 **straight**   immediately

24 **trim her up**   get her ready

25 **Hie**   hurry

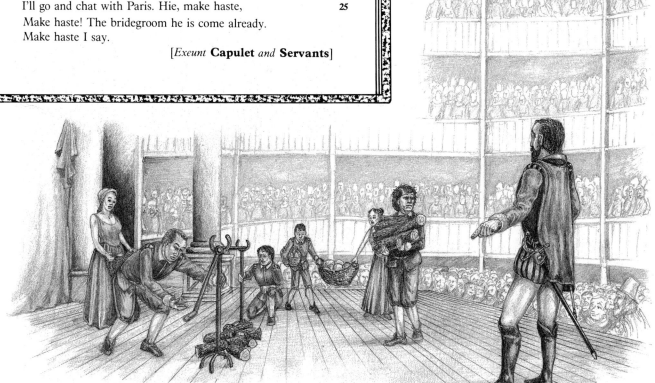

1   **Fast**   fast asleep
3   How do you think the Nurse should say this line?
    Practise it yourself.
4   **pennyworths**   small quantities (that is, naps)
6   **set up his rest**   determined
    The Nurse indulges in the same kind of bawdy
    double-meaning that she did when talking of
    Romeo. (See the final lines of Act II Scene 5.)
7   Why do you think the Nurse says **God forgive
    me!**?
12   **down**   laid down
15   **weraday**   alas
16   **aqua-vitae**   brandy (or other spirit-based liquor)

Scene 5

The same.

Nurse   [*Going to curtains*] Mistress! What, mistress! Juliet! Fast,
    I warrant her, she.
  Why, lamb, why, lady, fie! You slug-abed!
  Why, love I say! Madam! Sweetheart! Why, bride!
  What, not a word? You take your pennyworths now.
  Sleep for a week; for the next night, I warrant,   5
  The County Paris hath set up his rest
  That you shall rest but little! God forgive me!
  Marry and amen. How sound is she asleep!
  I needs must wake her. Madam, madam, madam!
  Ay, let the County take you in your bed,   10
  He'll fright you up, i'faith. Will it not be?
  What, dressed, and in your clothes, and down again?
  I must needs wake you. Lady! Lady! Lady!
  Alas, alas! Help, help! My lady's dead!
  O weraday that ever I was born.   15
  Some aqua-vitae, ho! My lord! My lady!

[*Enter* **Lady Capulet**]

Lady Capulet   What noise is here?

Nurse   O lamentable day!

Lady Capulet   What is the matter?

Nurse   Look, look! O heavy day!

Lady Capulet   O me, O me! My child, my only life.
  Revive, look up, or I will die with thee.   20
  Help, help! Call help!

[*Enter* **Capulet**]

Capulet   For shame, bring Juliet forth, her lord is come.

Nurse   She's dead, deceased! She's dead! Alack the day!

Lady Capulet   Alack the day! She's dead, she's dead, she's
  dead!

O me, O me! My child, my only life.

Royal Shakespeare Company 1976

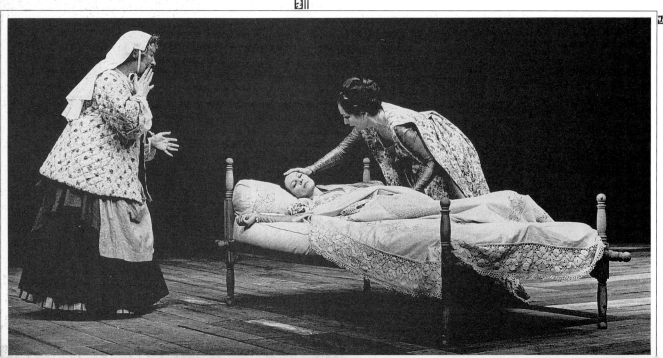

Capulet   Ha! Let me see her. Out alas. She's cold,   25
Her blood is settled and her joints are stiff.
Life and these lips have long been separated.
Death lies on her like an untimely frost
Upon the sweetest flower of all the field.

Nurse   O lamentable day!

Lady Capulet   O woeful time!   30

Capulet   Death, that hath ta'en her hence to make me wail
Ties up my tongue and will not let me speak.

[*Enter* **Friar Laurence** *and* **Paris** *and* **Musicians**]

Friar Laurence   Come, is the bride ready to go to church?

Capulet   Ready to go, but never to return.
O son, the night before thy wedding day   35
Hath Death lain with thy wife. There she lies,
Flower as she was, deflowerèd by him.
Death is my son-in-law, Death is my heir.
My daughter he hath wedded. I will die,
And leave him all: life, living, all is Death's.   40

Paris   Have I thought long to see this morning's face,
And doth it give me such a sight as this?

Lady Capulet   Accursed, unhappy, wretched, hateful day.
Most miserable hour that e'er time saw
In lasting labour of his pilgrimage.   45
But one, poor one, one poor and loving child,
But one thing to rejoice and solace in,
And cruel Death hath catched it from my sight.

Nurse   O woe! O woeful, woeful, woeful day.
Most lamentable day. Most woeful day   50
That ever, ever I did yet behold.
O day, O day, O day, O hateful day.
Never was seen so black a day as this.
O woeful day, O woeful day.

Paris   Beguiled, divorced, wronged, spited, slain.   55
Most detestable Death, by thee beguiled,

25 **Out**   an expression of lament
25-7 **she's cold . . . separated**   See Act IV Scene 1
lines 95–103.
26 **is settled**   that is, there is no pulse
28 **untimely**   unseasonal (as in Capulet's **frost/Upon
the sweetest flower**, which presumably is
blooming in spring or summer)
31 **ta'en**   taken
36-7   The idea of Death personified as Juliet's lover is
raised in the play three times before and once after
this. Find these references. What is the effect of the
recurrence of this theme?
37 **deflowerèd**   her virginity taken
40 **living**   property
(See **Death is my heir**, line 38.)
41 **long**   for a long time
45 **lasting labour**   unceasing toil
Why do you think the eternal passage of time is
seen as a **pilgrimage**?
46 **But**   I only possessed
47 **solace**   take comfort
48 **catched**   snatched
55 **Beguiled**   deceived

Royal Shakespeare Company 1967

58 Not life ... death although not alive, still my love
60 Uncomfortable discomforting
61 solemnity (marriage) ceremony
55-61 Closely examine these lines. In what way may they be said to be essentially selfish?
65-6 Confusion's cure ... confusions the remedy for calamity does not exist in making these outbursts
67 part a share in
maid The Friar knows, of course, that she is in fact already married to Romeo.
69 Your part that is, her mortal body
70 his part that is, her immortal soul
71 promotion advancement to the happiest possible state (of an advantageous marriage)
72 your heaven your idea of heaven
73 Upon which word in this line do you think the actor should place particular emphasis?
73-4 See *Twelfth Night*, Act I Scene 5 lines 64–78.
75 this love that is, your earthly love
79 rosemary This herb was a symbol of remembrance carried, as here, at weddings, but also at funerals. (See *Hamlet*, Act IV Scene 5 lines 172-3.)
80-1 See Act IV Scene 1 lines 109–12. So far the Friar's scheme is going according to plan.
82 fond The word at this time usually meant 'foolish' or 'weak', although there is a hint of the modern meaning here.
nature natural affection
83 Our heart makes us shed tears which our head tells us are causes for good cheer.
84 ordainèd festival determined for festive purposes
85 Turn the word is here used as an imperative, not as a description.
office function
86 instruments that is, musical instruments
87 cheer banquet
88 solemn ceremonial

By cruel, cruel thee quite overthrown.
O love! O life! Not life, but love in death!

Capulet   Despised, distressed, hated, martyred, killed.
Uncomfortable time, why cam'st thou now   60
To murder, murder our solemnity?
O child, O child! My soul and not my child,
Dead art thou. Alack, my child is dead,
And with my child my joys are buried.

Friar Laurence   Peace, ho, for shame. Confusion's cure lives not   65
In these confusions. Heaven and yourself
Had part in this fair maid, now heaven hath all,
And all the better is it for the maid.
Your part in her you could not keep from death,
But heaven keeps his part in eternal life.   70
The most you sought was her promotion,
For 'twas your heaven she should be advanced,
And weep ye now, seeing she is advanced
Above the clouds, as high as heaven itself?
O, in this love you love your child so ill   75
That you run mad, seeing that she is well.
She's not well married that lives married long,
But she's best married that dies married young.
Dry up your tears, and stick your rosemary
On this fair corse, and, as the custom is,   80
All in her best array bear her to church.
For though fond nature bids us all lament,
Yet nature's tears are reason's merriment.

Capulet   All things that we ordainèd festival
Turn from their office to black funeral: 85
Our instruments to melancholy bells,
Our wedding cheer to a sad burial feast;
Our solemn hymns to sullen dirges change,
Our bridal flowers serve for a buried corse,
And all things change them to the contrary.   90

Royal Shakespeare Company 1989

Friar Laurence   Sir, go you in, and madam, go with him,
And go, Sir Paris. Every one prepare
To follow this fair corse unto her grave.
The heavens do lour upon you for some ill;
Move them no more by crossing their high will.   95
  [*Exeunt all but the* **Nurse** *and* **Musicians**, *casting rosemary
    on* **Juliet** *and shutting the curtains*]

1st Musician   Faith, we may put up our pipes and be gone.

Nurse   Honest good fellows, ah put up, put up,
For well you know this is a pitiful case.

1st Musician   Ay, by my troth, the case may be amended.
                                          [*Exit* **Nurse**]

[*Enter* **Peter**]

Peter   Musicians, O musicians, 'Heart's ease', 'Heart's ease'!   100
O, and you will have me live, play 'Heart's ease'.

1st Musician   Why 'Heart's ease'?

Peter   O musicians, because my heart itself plays 'My heart
is full'. O play me some merry dump to comfort me.

1st Musician   Not a dump we! 'Tis no time to play now.   105

Peter   You will not then?

1st Musician   No.

---

94   **lour**   look angry, frown
95   **Move**   anger
96   **put**   pack
99   **by my troth**   as I am telling the truth (a very mild oath)
     the case may be amended   (i) the state of affairs may be made better (picking up the Nurse's meaning in the previous line); (ii) my instrument case may be mended
100   **Heart's ease**   a popular song of the time
101   **and you . . . live**   if you want me to stay alive
103–4   **My heart is full**   probably the title or a line from another popular song
104   **dump**   a sad tune
     Merry dump   is, of course, a contradiction in terms. The technical name for such a phrase is an 'oxymoron'.

O play me some merry dump to comfort me

Crucible Theatre 1984

108 give it you pay you out
soundly thoroughly (with a double meaning – can you spot it?)
110 gleek contemptuous gesture
To call someone a **minstrel** was contemptuous, because by an Act of Parliament of 1572 minstrels were considered as vagabonds.
112 give call
serving-creature a term even more contemptuous than 'servant' or 'serving-man'
114 pate head
carry no crotchets put up with no airs (with a musical pun)
114– re ... fa ... Peter puns on the second and fourth
15 notes in the musical scale, 'ray' or 'beray' meaning 'befoul', and 'fay' meaning 'clear away filth'.
115 note take note of (with obvious musical pun)
116 you note us (i) you set us to music; (ii) *you* will have to take note of *us*
117 up away
put out display
119 have at I attack (a fencing term)
dry-beat severely beat
122–4/ the opening lines of another popular song of the
136–7 time
126/ **Catling ... Rebeck ... Soundpost** all names of
128/ contemporary string instruments (which suggests
131 that **pipes** in line 96 is not to be taken literally)
129 silver ... sound punning on the sense of silver coins chinking together
129– sound for silver play for money
30
133 cry you mercy beg your pardon
133–4 you are ... you Displaying his **iron wit**, Peter pretends to apologise for asking the singer to speak, on the grounds that as a singer he cannot be exected to *speak*.
135 have ... sounding (i) do not receive gold for their music-making; (ii) have no gold with which to make a chinking noise in their pockets
137 lend redress give compensation
139 Jack knave, low fellow
in go in, stay in (Capulet's house)
tarry wait
140 stay wait for

What dramatic purpose is served by the interlude with the musicians?

Romeo has been absent for the whole of Act IV. Shakespeare often takes his main actor off stage during the third quarter of a play. Why?

Peter   I will then give it you soundly.

1st Musician   What will you give us?

Peter   No money, on my faith, but the gleek! I will give you   110
the minstrel.

1st Musician   Then will I give you the serving-creature.

Peter   Then will I lay the serving-creature's dagger on your
pate. I will carry no crotchets. I'll re you, I'll fa you. Do
you note me?   115

1st Musician   And you re us and fa us, you note us.

2nd Musician   Pray you put up your dagger and put out your
wit.

Peter   Then have at you with my wit. I will dry-beat you
with an iron wit, and put up my iron dagger. Answer me   120
like men.
'When griping griefs the hearth doth wound,
And doleful dumps the mind oppress,
Then music with her silver sound' –
Why 'silver sound'? Why 'music with her silver sound'?   125
What say you, Simon Catling?

1st Musician   Marry, sir, because silver hath a sweet sound.

Peter   Pretty! What say you, Hugh Rebeck?

2nd Musician   I say 'silver sound' because musicians sound
for silver.   130

Peter   Prates too. What say you, James Soundpost?

3rd Musician   Faith, I know not what to say.

Peter   O, I cry you mercy, you are the singer. I will say for
you. It is 'music with her silver sound' because musicians
have no gold for sounding.   135
'Then music with her silver sound
With speedy help doth lend redress.'   [*Exit*]

1st Musician   What a pestilent knave is this same.

2nd Musician   Hang him, Jack. Come, we'll in here, tarry for
the mourners, and stay dinner.   140

[*Exeunt*]

Act V

Scene 1

A street in Mantua. Enter **Romeo**.

Romeo　If I may trust the flattering truth of sleep
　　My dreams presage some joyful news at hand.
　　My bosom's lord sits lightly in his throne
　　And all this day an unaccustomed spirit
　　Lifts me above the ground with cheerful thoughts.　　5
　　I dreamt my lady came and found me dead –
　　Strange dream that gives a dead man leave to think! –
　　And breathed such life with kisses in my lips
　　That I revived and was an emperor.
　　Ah me, how sweet is love itself possessed　　10
　　When but love's shadows are so rich in joy.

[*Enter* **Balthasar**, *Romeo's* **servant**, *booted*]

　　News from Verona! How, now Balthasar,
　　Dost thou not bring me letters from the Friar?
　　How doth my lady? Is my father well?
　　How doth my Juliet? That I ask again,　　15
　　For nothing can be ill if she be well.

Balthasar　Then she is well and nothing can be ill.
　　Her body sleeps in Capels' monument,
　　And her immortal part with angels lives.
　　I saw her laid low in her kindred's vault　　20
　　And presently took post to tell it you.
　　O pardon me for bringing these ill news,
　　Since you did leave it for my office, sir.

Romeo　Is it e'en so? Then I defy you, stars!
　　Thou know'st my lodging. Get me ink and paper,　　25
　　And hire posthorses. I will hence tonight.

1　**flattering . . . sleep** It was supposed that revelations of truth sometimes came during sleep.
2　**presage** predict
3　**bosom's lord** that is, love (or Cupid, the god of love)
　　lightly cheerfully
　　throne that is, the heart
4　**spirit** in this case, high spirits
6　Can you find premonitions of death from earlier in the play?
7　**leave** permission
10　**possessed** in reality
11　**but love's shadows** only the shadows (that is, dreams) of love
SD　**booted** wearing riding boots
　　Why do you think that this, one of the original stage directions, was put into the text?
14　**lady** Juliet (not Romeo's mother – see the following two lines)
18　**monument** burial vault
21　**presently took post** immediately set out with post-horses
23　**for my office** as my duty (that is, bringing Romeo all the news)
24　**e'en** even
26　**post-horses** horses at an inn available for hire by travellers or post-riders

Zeffirelli 1968

27 patience fortitude
28 import imply
34 lie with usually in the sense of a lover, but here in death
35 see for means consider the way (of killing myself)
38 'a he
which late I noted whom I recently noticed
39 weeds clothes
overwhelming overhanging
40 Culling of simples gathering medicinal herbs
Of whom does this remind us, and why is such a reminder ironic?
Meagre thin
42 needy poor
45 beggarly account wretchedly poor store
46 earthen earthenware
bladders used for storing liquids
47 packthread strong twine used for tying parcels or bundles
cakes of roses rose petals compressed into cakes for use as perfume; (**old** implies that they have long since lost their effect)
50 And if if
51 the penalty for the sale of which is immediate death in Mantua (but not, apparently, in England)
52 caitiff miserable, pitiable
would willing to
53 but forerun merely anticipate
What do you think has crossed Romeo's mind before Balthasar brings his news?
54 needy punning on the previous line

Re-read lines 1–48. What differing states of mind does Romeo show in this passage?

Why does Shakespeare give the lengthy description of the apothecary (lines 37–48)?

Balthasar   I do beseech you sir, have patience.
Your looks are pale and wild and do import
Some misadventure.

Romeo   Tush, thou art deceived.
Leave me, and do the thing I bid thee do.   30
Hast thou no letters to me from the Friar?

Balthasar   No, my good lord.

Romeo   No matter. Get thee gone.
And hire those horses. I'll be with thee straight.

                         [*Exit* **Balthasar**]

Well, Juliet, I will lie with thee tonight.
Let's see for means. O mischief thou art swift   35
To enter in the thoughts of desperate men.
I do remember an apothecary –
And hereabouts 'a dwells – which late I noted
In tattered weeds, with overwhelming brows,
Culling of simples. Meagre were his looks,   40
Sharp misery had worn him to the bones,
And in his needy shop a tortoise hung,
An alligator stuffed, and other skins
Of ill-shaped fishes; and about his shelves
A beggarly account of empty boxes,   45
Green earthen pots, bladders, and musty seeds,
Remnants of packthread, and old cakes of roses
Were thinly scattered to make up a show.
Noting this penury, to myself I said,
'And if a man did need a poison now,   50
Whose sale is present death in Mantua,
Here lives a caitiff wretch would sell it him'.
O, this same thought did but forerun my need,
And this same needy man must sell it me.
As I remember, this should be the house.   55

This is an eighteenth-century print of an apothecary's shop. Do you think the apothecary in the play had such a prosperous-looking set-up? Re-read lines 37–48. Draw a sketch of Romeo's apothecary and his shop.

Being holiday, the beggar's shop is shut.
What ho! Apothecary!

[*Enter* **Apothecary**]

Apothecary   Who calls so loud?

Romeo   Come hither, man. I see that thou art poor.
Hold, there is forty ducats. Let me have
A dram of poison, such soon-speeding gear   60
As will disperse itself through all the veins,
That the life-weary taker may fall dead,
And that the trunk may be discharged of breath
As violently as hasty powder fired
Doth hurry from the fatal cannon's womb.   65

Apothecary   Such mortal drugs I have, but Mantua's law
Is death to any he that utters them.

Romeo   Art thou so bare and full of wretchedness,
And fear'st to die? Famine is in thy cheeks,
Need and oppression starveth in thy eyes,   70
Contempt and beggary hangs upon thy back.
The world is not thy friend, nor the world's law;
The world affords no law to make thee rich;
Then be not poor, but break it, and take this.

Apothecary   My poverty, but not my will consents.   75

Romeo   I pay thy poverty and not thy will.

Apothecary   [*Giving* **Romeo** *a vial of poison*] Put this in any
liquid thing you will
And drink it off and if you had the strength
Of twenty men it would dispatch you straight.

Romeo   There is thy gold – worse poison to men's souls,   80
Doing more murder in this loathsome world
Than these poor compounds that thou mayst not sell.
I sell thee poison, thou hast sold me none.
Farewell, buy food, and get thyself in flesh.
Come, cordial, and not poison, go with me   85
To Juliet's grave, for there must I use thee.   [*Exeunt*]

59 **ducats** A ducat was a gold coin, and forty ducats represents a considerable sum of money.
60 **dram** dose
   soon-speeding gear quick-working stuff
63 **trunk** body
64 **hasty powder** volatile gunpowder
   Compare the imagery in lines 64–5 with Act II Scene 6 lines 9–10 and Act III Scene 3 lines 131–2.
66 **mortal** deadly
67 **utters** sells
68 **bare** poor
70 the starving effect of oppressive need is reflected in your eyes
71 **Contempt and beggary** contemptible beggary
   This device of using two words joined by 'and' for one idea is known as 'hendiadys', (e.g. 'goblets and gold' for 'golden goblets').
   hangs that is, in tatters
73 **affords** offers
74 **it** that is, the law
   this that is, the money offered
75 **consents** makes me agree to your proposition
79 **dispatch** literally, send your soul away; that is, kill
85 **cordial** medicine (originally one that stimulated the heart) Do you think there is any intended irony here?

David Threlfall as Smike playing the Apothecary, and Roger Rees as Nicholas Nickleby playing Romeo, in *The Life and Adventures of Nicholas Nickleby*, adapted from Dickens by David Edgar.

Royal Shakespeare Company 1980

1 **brother** a familiar name between friars
2 **should** must
4 **his mind be writ** he has written down his
   thoughts
5–6 **barefoot brother . . . order** Franciscan friars went
   barefoot.
6 **associate** accompany
   It was a rule of the Franciscan order that brothers
   must travel in pairs as a check on each other's
   behaviour.
8 **searchers** health officers whose job it was to view
   dead bodies and report on the cause of death
9 **house** It is not clear whether this is a domestic
   dwelling or a religious house such as a monastery.
10 **pestilence** plague
   reign prevail
11 **Sealed up the doors** a common practice during
   times of plague
12 **stayed** halted
5–12 These lines are confused, and the syntax does not
   make good sense. What do you think this shows us
   about Friar John's state of mind?
13 **bare** carried
17 **brotherhood** that is, the Franciscan order
18 **nice** trivial
   charge important matter
19 **dear import** serious importance
21 **crow** crowbar
25 **beshrew** blame
26 **accidents** happenings

> Find out as much as you can about the
> plague, of which there were frequent out-
> breaks in London around the time when this
> play was written.

Scene 2

Verona. Friar Laurence's cell. Enter **Friar John**.

Friar John   Holy Franciscan Friar, Brother, ho!

[*Enter* **Friar Laurence**]

Friar Laurence   This same should be the voice of Friar John.
Welcome from Mantua. What says Romeo?
Or, if his mind be writ, give me his letter.

Friar John   Going to find a barefoot brother out,   5
One of our order, to associate me,
Here in this city visiting the sick,
And finding him, the searchers of the town,
Suspecting that we both were in a house
Where the infectious pestilence did reign,   10
Sealed up the doors and would not let us forth,
So that my speed to Mantua there was stayed.

Friar Laurence   Who bare my letter then to Romeo?

Friar John   I could not send it – here it is again –
Nor get a messenger to bring it thee,   15
So fearful were they of infection.

Friar Laurence   Unhappy fortune! By my brotherhood,
The letter was not nice but full of charge,
Of dear import, and the neglecting it
May do much danger. Friar John, go hence,   20
Get me an iron crow and bring it straight
Unto my cell.

Friar John   Brother, I'll go and bring it thee.   [*Exit*]

Friar Laurence   Now must I to the monument alone.
Within this three hours will fair Juliet wake.
She will beshrew me much that Romeo   25
Hath had no notice of these accidents,
But I will write again to Mantua,
And keep her at my cell till Romeo come.
Poor living corse, closed in a dead man's tomb.   [*Exit*]

I could not send it – here it is again –

Redgrave Theatre 1974

Scene 3

Verona. A churchyard, within which is a tomb belonging to the
Capulets. Enter **Paris** *and his* **Page**, *with flowers and sweet water.*

Paris   Give me thy torch, boy. Hence and stand aloof.
Yet put it out, for I would not be seen.
Under yond yew trees lay thee all along,
Holding thy ear close to the hollow ground;
So shall no foot upon the churchyard tread,   5
Being loose, unfirm, with digging up of graves,
But thou shalt hear it. Whistle then to me
As signal that thou hear'st something approach.
Give me those flowers. Do as I bid thee. Go.

Page   I am almost afraid to stand alone   10
Here in the churchyard. Yet I will adventure.   [*Retires*]
                              [**Paris** *strews the tomb with flowers*]

Paris   Sweet flower, with flowers thy bridal bed I strew.
O woe, thy canopy is dust and stones
Which with sweet water nightly I will dew,
Or wanting that, with tears distilled by moans.   15
The obsequies that I for thee will keep
Nightly shall be to strew thy grave and weep.
                                            [**Page** *whistles*]
The boy gives warning something doth approach.
What cursed foot wanders this way tonight,
To cross my obsequies and true love's rite?   20
What, with a torch? Muffle me, night, awhile.
                              [**Paris** *steps back into shadows*]

[*Enter* **Romeo** *and* **Balthasar** *with a torch, a mattock and a crow*
of iron]

SD *sweet*   perfumed
 1 **Hence . . . aloof**   go and stay at a distance
 3 **all along**   flat on the ground
 4 **hollow**   echoing
11 **adventure**   risk it
12 **Sweet flower**   that is, Juliet
Compare this line with *Hamlet*, Act V Scene 1 line
237, where Gertrude strews flowers on Ophelia's
grave.
13 **canopy**   covering
Juliet might have expected to have a canopy of rich
fabric over her four-poster wedding bed; but
instead she has a stone vault. With this in mind,
turn back to Act III Scene 5 and find a line said by
Lady Capulet which now becomes highly ironic.
15 **wanting**   lacking
    distilled by   extracted from
16 **obsequies**   funeral rites
    keep   regularly observe
20 **cross**   thwart, interrupt
SD *mattock*   a kind of pick-axe

Paris' lament in lines 12–17 is formal and
rhyming. It is a perfect sestet, that is, the first
six lines of a sonnet; and the fourteen-line
sonnet was the form conventionally used
when composing a poem to a loved one.
Does this tell you anything about the true
nature of Paris' grief? Compare these lines
with Romeo's lament later in this scene.

Give me thy torch, boy. Hence and
stand aloof.

Redgrave Theatre 1974

23 **letter** See Act V Scene 1 line 23.
25 **charge** command
26 **stand all aloof** Note the parallel with line 1.
27 **course** that is, course of action
30–1 **But chiefly . . . precious ring** Is Romeo telling the truth at this moment, or is it merely a pretence for Balthasar's benefit to cover his intended suicide?
32 **dear** personally important
33 **jealous** suspicious
34 **In** into
36 **hungry** because Death is greedy for bodies
43 **For all this same** despite all this
44 **doubt** suspect
45 **maw** stomach
      womb belly
46 **dearest morsel** that is, Juliet
48 **in despite** to defy thee
52 **villainous shame** What could be in Paris' mind?
53 **apprehend** arrest

Romeo   Give me that mattock and the wrenching iron.
Hold, take this letter. Early in the morning
See thou deliver it to my lord and father.
Give me the light. Upon thy life I charge thee,   25
Whate'er thou hear'st or seest, stand all aloof
And do not interrupt me in my course.
Why I descend into this bed of death
Is partly to behold my lady's face
But chiefly to take thence from her dead finger   30
A precious ring, a ring that I must use
In dear employment. Therefore hence, be gone.
But if thou jealous dost return to pry
In what I farther shall intend to do,
By heaven I will tear thee joint by joint,   35
And strew this hungry churchyard with thy limbs.
The time and my intents are savage-wild,
More fierce and more inexorable far
Than empty tigers or the roaring sea.

Balthasar   I will be gone, sir, and not trouble ye.   40

Romeo   So shalt thou show me friendship. Take thou that.
                              [**Romeo** *gives him his purse*]
Live, and be prosperous, and farewell, good fellow.

Balthasar   For all this same, I'll hide me hereabout.
His looks I fear, and his intents I doubt.
                  [**Balthasar** *retires and hides in the churchyard*]

Romeo   Thou detestable maw, thou womb of death   45
Gorged with the dearest morsel of the earth,
Thus I enforce thy rotten jaws to open,
And in despite I'll cram thee with more food.
                              [**Romeo** *breaks open the tomb*]

Paris   This is that banished haughty Montague
That murdered my love's cousin – with which grief   50
It is supposed the fair creature died –
And here is come to do some villainous shame
To the dead bodies. I will apprehend him.
Stop thy unhallowed toil, vile Montague.

Thus I enforce thy rotten jaws to open

Crucible Theatre 1984

Can vengeance be pursued further than death?   55
Condemned villain, I do apprehend thee.
Obey, and go with me, for thou must die.

Romeo   I must indeed, and therefore came I hither.
Good gentle youth, tempt not a desperate man.
Fly hence and leave me. Think upon these gone.   60
Let them affright thee. I beseech thee, youth,
Put not another sin upon my head
By urging me to fury. O be gone.
By heaven I love thee better than myself,
For I come hither armed against myself.   65
Stay not, be gone, live, and hereafter say
A mad man's mercy bid thee run away.

Paris   I do defy thy conjuration
And apprehend thee for a felon here.

Romeo   Wilt thou provoke me? Then have at thee, boy!   70
[They fight]

Page   O Lord, they fight! I will go call the Watch.
*[Exit **Page**]*

Paris   O, I am slain! If thou be merciful,
Open the tomb, lay me with Juliet.   *[**Paris** dies]*

Romeo   In faith I will. Let me peruse this face.
Mercutio's kinsman, noble County Paris!   75
What said my man, when my betossed soul
Did not attend him, as we rode? I think
He told me Paris should have married Juliet.
Said he not so? Or did I dream it so?
Or am I mad, hearing him talk of Juliet,   80
To think it was so? O, give me thy hand,
One writ with me in sour misfortune's book.
I'll bury thee in a triumphant grave.
A grave? O no, a lantern, slaughtered youth.
For here lies Juliet, and her beauty makes   85
This vault a feasting presence, full of light.
Death, lie thou there, by a dead man interred.
How oft when men are at the point of death

59   **youth** In the darkness Romeo does not recognise Paris.
60   **these gone** the dead who lie around them
65   What is it that Romeo has brought as a weapon 'against himself'?
68   **conjuration** solemn appeal
69   **for** as
70   **have at thee** a fencing term warning of imminent attack
71   **Watch** a small band of ordinary citizens who came together each night in order to patrol the streets and keep the peace
(Remember that at this time there was no regular police force.)
76   **betossed soul** turbulent mind
77   **attend** pay attention to
78   **should have** was to have
82   **One writ with me** a person written down alongside myself
83   **triumphant** glorious
84   **lantern** in architecture, a turret full of windows which illuminates the inside of a building
85   It is possible that Juliet may be lying on her tomb in exactly the same position as she was on her bed in Act IV Scene 3. What is the effect of such a 'double image'?
86   **feasting** that is, appearing full of light (and thus decorated) as if during festival time
presence a special room in a palace where monarchs gave audience to visitors (Juliet is the monarch here)
87   **Death . . . a dead man** the body of Paris . . . Romeo (soon himself to be dead)
Where do you suppose Romeo lays Paris' body?

Said he not so? Or did I dream it so?

Royal Shakespeare Company 1989

89 **keepers** (i) nurses; (ii) jailors
90 **lightning** It has been noticed that people sometimes experience a revival of their spirits shortly before death.
91 **this** this situation
94 **ensign** flag
 With what do you think Romeo is comparing what has happened to Juliet? What is the likely effect on the audience of the comparison in these three lines?
97 **sheet** winding-sheet or shroud in which corpses were wrapped (see Act IV Scene 3 lines 42-3)
99 **twain** two
100 **sunder his that** cut in two the youth of he who
101 Why does Romeo call Tybalt **cousin**?
101-2 **Ah ... fair** The dramatic irony here is painful because we, the audience, know why.
103 **unsubstantial** having no body
102-5 **Shall I believe ... paramour** Find other places where Death is seen as Juliet's lover.
106 **still** always
109 See *Hamlet*, Act IV Scene 3 lines 20-2.
111 **inauspicious stars** stars which were against me from my birth
115 an everlasting agreement with all-devouring Death
116 **conduct** that is, the poison
118 **dashing rocks** rocks which dash to pieces
 bark boat (that is, his body)
119 **Here's to my love** Find the words in Act IV Scene 3 which parallel Romeo's words here.
120 **quick** (i) quick-acting; (ii) life-giving
 In what way do you think Romeo might intend the second meaning?
121 **speed** protector
122 **stumbled at graves** supposed to be a bad omen
 at over

Describe in detail the actions of the actor playing Romeo as they are dictated to him by lines 112-20.

Enter Friar Laurence

Lyceum Theatre 1882

Have they been merry! Which their keepers call
A lightning before death. O how may I   90
Call this a lightning? O my love, my wife,
Death that hath sucked the honey of thy breath
Hath had no power yet upon thy beauty.
Thou art not conquered. Beauty's ensign yet
Is crimson in thy lips and in thy cheeks,   95
And Death's pale flag is not advanced there.
Tybalt, liest thou there in thy bloody sheet?
O, what more favour can I do to thee
Than with that hand that cut thy youth in twain
To sunder his that was thine enemy?   100
Forgive me, cousin. Ah, dear Juliet,
Why art thou yet so fair? Shall I believe
That unsubstantial Death is amorous,
And that the lean abhorred monster keeps
Thee here in dark to be his paramour?   105
For fear of that I still will stay with thee,
And never from this palace of dim night
Depart again. Here, here, will I remain
With worms that are thy chambermaids. O here
Will I set up my everlasting rest   110
And shake the yoke of inauspicious stars
From this world-wearied flesh. Eyes, look your last.
Arms, take your last embrace! And lips, O you
The doors of breath, seal with a righteous kiss
A dateless bargain to engrossing Death   115
Come, bitter conduct, come unsavoury guide,
Thou desperate pilot now at once run on
The dashing rocks thy seasick weary bark.
Here's to my love! [*He drinks*] O true apothecary,
Thy drugs are quick. Thus with a kiss I die.   120
                                              [*He falls*]

[*Enter* **Friar Laurence**, *with lantern, crow and spade*]

Friar Laurence Saint Francis be my speed. How oft tonight
 Have my old feet stumbled at graves. Who's there?

Balthasar   Here's one, a friend, and one that knows you well.

Friar Laurence   Bliss be upon you. Tell me, good my friend,
What torch is yond that vainly lends his light   **125**
To grubs and eyeless skulls? As I discern,
It burneth in the Capels' monument.

Balthasar   It doth so, holy sir, and there's my master,
One that you love.

Friar Laurence   Who is it?

Balthasar   Romeo.

Friar Laurence   How long hath he been there?

Balthasar   Full half an hour. **130**

Friar Laurence   Go with me to the vault.

Balthasar   I dare not, sir.
My master knows not but I am gone hence,
And fearfully did menace me with death
If I did stay to look on his intents.

Friar Laurence   Stay then, I'll go alone. Fear comes upon me. **135**
O, much I fear some ill unthrifty thing.

Balthasar   As I did sleep under this yew tree here
I dreamt my master and another fought,
And that my master slew him.

Friar Laurence   Romeo!
       [*He stoops and looks on the blood and weapons*]
Alack, alack, what blood is this which stains   **140**
The stony entrance of this sepulchre?
What mean these masterless and gory swords
To lie discoloured by this place of peace?

[*He enters the vault*]

Romeo! O, pale! Who else? What, Paris too?
And steeped in blood? Ah what an unkind hour   **145**
Is guilty of this lamentable chance?
The lady stirs.

[**Juliet** *rises*]

---

125 **vainly** in vain, uselessly
126 **grubs** worms
132 **knows not but** is under the impression that
136 **unthrifty** unfortunate
137–9 Do you think Balthasar was dreaming? Or did he
      actually see what happened and is too frightened
      to say so?
142 **masterless** ownerless
145 **unkind** unnatural

> Re-read lines 45–120. Consider (a) presentation of character, (b) dramatic qualities and (c) poetic qualities.

Theatre Royal, Covent Garden 1784

In the eighteenth century tragic endings were considered unsophisticated, and the conclusion of *Romeo and Juliet* was rewritten with a sentimental ending. What is your opinion of this practice? Decide where you think the line in the caption to this picture would have come in the text (assuming it to be the first line of a changed ending). Go on to write that ending – you need not reproduce blank verse lines.

Mr. HOLMAN in the CHARACTER of ROMEO.

She speaks! She lives! and we shall still be blessed!

Act 5.th Scene the last.

148 **comfortable** comforting
150 **Where is my Romeo?** In view of line 155, Juliet must still be confused as she awakes from her drugged sleep.
152 **unnatural sleep** that is, death
156 **dispose** place
159 Do you think the Friar's fear and desire to escape is consistent with his character as already established?
162 **timeless** (i) untimely; (ii) eternal
163 **churl** thoughtless man (originally, bad-mannered rustic)
165 **Haply** perhaps
166 **restorative** that is, her kiss which will be a cure because it will kill her and thus restore her to Romeo
169 **happy** (i) opportunely found; (ii) fortunate in being the means of reuniting her with Romeo
170 **This** Juliet's bosom
 rust Some editors prefer the first quarto reading of 'rest'. Which do you think is more poetic?
173 **attach** arrest

Juliet   O comfortable Friar, where is my lord?
 I do remember well where I should be,
 And there I am. Where is my Romeo?   150

Friar Laurence   I hear some noise. Lady, come from that nest
 Of death, contagion, and unnatural sleep.
 A greater power than we can contradict
 Hath thwarted our intents. Come, come away.
 Thy husband in thy bosom there lies dead,   155
 And Paris too. Come, I'll dispose of thee
 Among a sisterhood of holy nuns.
 Stay not to question, for the Watch is coming.
 Come, go, good Juliet. I dare no longer stay.

Juliet   Go, get thee hence, for I will not away.   160
                    [*Exit* **Friar Laurence**]
 What's here? A cup closed in my true love's hand?
 Poison, I see, hath been his timeless end.
 O churl. Drunk all, and left no friendly drop
 To help me after? I will kiss thy lips.
 Haply some poison yet doth hang on them   165
 To make me die with a restorative.   [*She kisses him*]
 Thy lips are warm!

Watchman   [*Within*] Lead, boy. Which way?

Juliet   Yea, noise? Then I'll be brief. O happy dagger.
 This is thy sheath. There rust, and let me die.   170
                    [*She stabs herself and falls*]

[*Enter* **Page** *and* **Watchmen**]

Page   This is the place. There, where the torch doth burn.

Watchman   The ground is bloody. Search about the
    churchyard.
 Go, some of you: whoe'er you find, attach.
                    [*Exeunt some* **Watchmen**]
 Pitiful sight! Here lies the County slain
 And Juliet bleeding, warm, and newly dead,   175
 Who here hath lain this two days buried.
 Go tell the Prince. Run to the Capulets.
 Raise up the Montagues. Some others search.

Compare the Friar's words as he faces actual disaster with his more formal words at the supposed death of Juliet in Act IV Scene 5.

In comparison with the men, all Shakespeare's dying women (with the exception of Cleopatra) have short final speeches. Can you find out anything about Elizabethan stage conditions which may account for this?

**I dare no longer stay.
Go, get thee hence, for I will not away.**

Bristol Old Vic 1966

[Exeunt some **Watchmen***]*

We see the ground whereon these woes do lie,
But the ground of all these piteous woes   180
We cannot without circumstance descry.

[Enter several **Watchmen** *with* **Balthasar***]*

2nd Watchman   Here's Romeo's man. We found him in the
      churchyard.

1st Watchman   Hold him in safety till the Prince come hither.

[Enter another **Watchman** *with* **Friar Laurence***]*

3rd Watchman   Here is a friar that trembles, sighs and weeps.
      We took this mattock and this spade from him   185
      As he was coming from this churchyard's side.

1st Watchman   A great suspicion. Stay the friar too.

[Enter the **Prince** *and* **Attendants***]*

Prince   What misadventure is so early up,
      That calls our person from our morning rest?

[Enter **Capulet** *and* **Lady Capulet***, and* **Servants***]*

Capulet   What should it be that is so shrieked abroad?   190

Lady Capulet   O, the people in the street cry 'Romeo',
      Some 'Juliet', and some 'Paris', and all run
      With open outcry toward our monument.

Prince   What fear is this which startles in our ears?

1st Watchman   Sovereign, here lies the County Paris slain, 195
      And Romeo dead, and Juliet, dead before,
      Warm, and new killed.

Prince   Search, seek, and know how this foul murder comes.

1st Watchman   Here is a friar, and slaughtered Romeo's man,
      With instruments upon them fit to open   200
      These dead men's tombs.

Capulet   O heavens! O wife, look how our daughter bleeds!

179   **woes**   woeful creatures
180   **ground**   reason
      Explain clearly the punning which is going on in
      lines 179–80.
181   **without . . . descry**   work out without detailed
      information
183   **in safety**   under guard
186   **churchyard's side**   side of the churchyard
188   What unfortunate happening has occurred so early
      in the day?
190   **abroad**   in the streets
194   **startles**   makes a startling sound
198   **comes**   comes to be

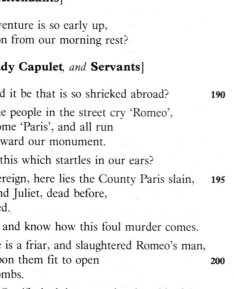

Poison, I see, hath been his timeless end.

Royal Shakespeare Company 1967

203 **mista'en** mistaken (its proper **house**; that is, its sheath on Romeo's back)
206 **bell** funeral bell
    Is she in fact old? See Act I Scene 3.
210 **liege** lord
    my wife ... tonight Shakespeare's acting company was not large, and it may have been that the actor who played Lady Montague was needed for another part in this scene. If so, Shakespeare has turned virtue to necessity and added an extra touch of pathos by making Montague doubly bereaved and quite alone – although it is a dramatic irony that he is not yet aware that Romeo too is dead.
214– Montague chides his unmannerly (**untaught**) son
15 who has died before him as he might push (**press**) in an ill-mannered fashion before his father into a room.
216 **mouth of outrage** expressions of passionate grief
218 **spring** source
219 **general** leader
220 **lead ... death** (i) go before you to my grave (out of grief); (ii) lead you to find and execute those who are responsible
    forbear restrain yourselves
221 **let ... patience** submit patiently to misfortune
222 **parties of** people under
223 **greatest** main suspect
    able to least Perhaps the Friar means that his age makes him the least likely to have caused the bloodshed.
224-5 **time ... against me** that is, the circumstantial evidence appears to implicate me
226 **impeach and purge** accuse and acquit
    Suggest one reason for condemning the Friar, and one reason for excusing him.
229 **date of breath** time left to live
233 **stolen** secret
234 **doomsday** day of death

Compare this point in the play in any way you find interesting with Act I Scene 1 lines 71–99 and Act III Scene 1 lines 135–95. Can you see any way in which the Prince gives the structure of the play a kind of symmetry?

This dagger hath mista'en, for lo, his house
Is empty on the back of Montague,
And it mis-sheathed in my daughter's bosom.   205

Lady Capulet   O me! This sight of death is as a bell
That warns my old age to a sepulchre.

[*Enter* **Montague** *and* **Servants**]

Prince   Come, Montague, for thou art early up
To see thy son and heir now early down.

Montague   Alas, my liege, my wife is dead tonight.   210
Grief of my son's exile hath stopped her breath.
What further woe conspires against mine age?

Prince   Look, and thou shalt see.

Montague   O thou untaught! What manners is in this,
To press before thy father to a grave?   215

Prince   Seal up the mouth of outrage for a while
Till we can clear these ambiguities
And know their spring, their head, their true descent,
And then will I be general of your woes
And lead you, even to death. Meantime forbear,   220
And let mischance be slave to patience.
Bring forth the parties of suspicion.

Friar Laurence   I am the greatest, able to do least,
Yet most suspected, as the time and place
Doth make against me, of this direful murder.   225
And here I stand, both to impeach and purge
Myself condemned and myself excused.

Prince   Then say at once what thou dost know in this.

Friar Laurence   I will be brief, for my short date of breath
Is not so long as is a tedious tale.   230
Romeo, there dead, was husband to that Juliet,
And she, there dead, that Romeo's faithful wife.
I married them, and their stol'n marriage day
Was Tybalt's doomsday, whose untimely death
Banished the new-made bridegroom from this city;   235
For whom, and not for Tybalt, Juliet pined.

Royal Shakespeare Company 1976

You, to remove that siege of grief from her,
Betrothed and would have married her perforce
To County Paris. Then comes she to me
And with wild looks bid me devise some mean   240
To rid her from this second marriage,
Or in my cell there would she kill herself.
Then gave I her – so tutored by my art –
A sleeping potion, which so took effect
As I intended, for it wrought on her   245
The form of death. Meantime I writ to Romeo
That he should hither come as this dire night
To help to take her from her borrowed grave,
Being the time the potion's force should cease.
But he which bore my letter, Friar John,   250
Was stayed by accident, and yesternight
Returned my letter back. Then all alone
At the prefixed hour of her waking
Came I to take her from her kindred's vault,
Meaning to keep her closely at my cell   255
Till I conveniently could send to Romeo.
But when I came, some minute ere the time
Of her awakening, here untimely lay
The noble Paris and true Romeo dead.
She wakes; and I entreated her come forth   260
And bear this work of heaven with patience,
But then a noise did scare me from the tomb
And she, too desperate, would not go with me
But, as it seems, did violence on herself.
All this I know; and to the marriage   265
Her Nurse is privy; and if aught in this
Miscarried by my fault, let my old life
Be sacrificed some hour before his time
Unto the rigour of severest law.

Prince   We still have known thee for a holy man.   270
Where's Romeo's man? What can he say to this?

Balthasar   I brought my master news of Juliet's death,
And then in post he came from Mantua
To this same place, to this same monument.

237 **You** Who is the Friar addressing? Would he point at the person? Is he accusing, aggressive, sorrowful, or a mixture of all?
237 **siege** assault
238 **Betrothed** pledged to marry
       perforce by compulsion
240 **mean** Nowadays we always use the plural 'means' even when referring to something singular.
243 **art** To what 'art' of his is he referring?
245-6 **wrought . . . form** created in her the outward appearance
247 **as** on
248 **borrowed** temporary
251 **stayed** delayed
253 **prefixed** pre-arranged
255 **closely** secretly
259 **true** faithful
260 **She wakes** What is the effect of the use of the present tense here?
       entreated begged
266 **privy** sharer in the secret
268 **his** its
270 **still** always
273 **in post** post haste, speedily

The Friar's long speech is often cut in performance. Why? Is anything lost by so doing?

Bristol Old Vic 1966

275 See lines 23-4 of this scene.
296 **going in**   as he went into
277 **If . . . not**   unless I departed
279 **raised**   alerted
280 **made your master**   was your master doing
284 **by and by**   at once
      drew   that is, drew his sword
286 **make good**   confirms
287 **tidings**   news
289 **Of**   from (*not* a misprint for the modern usage 'off')
      therewithal   with it (the poison)
292 **scourge**   punishment
293 **That**   so that
      joys   (i) happiness; (ii) children
      with love   because of their love for one another
294 **winking at**   shutting my eyes to, turning a blind eye to
295 **brace**   pair
      To whom is the Prince referring?
297 **This**   that is, my hand in reconciliation
      See the Prologue at the beginning of the play. In view of the ending of the family feuding, do you think Romeo and Juliet died uselessly?
      jointure   dowry, marriage settlement
299 **raise**   erect
      statue   Montague here means a recumbent effigy on her tomb (see **lie** at line 303).
300 **That whiles**   so that as long as
301 **at such rate be set**   be so highly (i) esteemed; (ii) valued
      Montague is talking of (i) the reputation of Juliet; (ii) the richness of her effigy.
303 There are many fine examples in English churches of Elizabethan effigies of man and wife lying side by side on their tomb. Do you know of any near you? If so, go and have a look at it.
304 **Poor sacrifices of**   (i) pitiful victims of; (ii) inadequate atonement for
305 **glooming**   overcast

Take lines 292-5 (**See what a scourge . . . punished**). Explain in detail to someone who does not know the play exactly to what the Prince is referring.

'Capulet, the Nurse and Friar Laurence all love Juliet, yet all help to bring about her death.' Consider any or all of these three in the light of this statement.

This letter he early bid me give his father   275
And threatened me with death, going in the vault,
If I departed not and left him there.

Prince   Give me the letter, I will look on it.
Where is the County's Page that raised the Watch?
Sirrah, what made your master in this place?   280

Page   He came with flowers to strew his lady's grave
And bid me stand aloof, and so I did.
Anon comes one with light to ope the tomb
And by and by my master drew on him,
And then I ran away to call the Watch.   285

Prince   This letter doth make good the Friar's words:
Their course of love, the tidings of her death,
And here he writes that he did buy a poison
Of a poor pothecary, and therewithal
Came to this vault to die and lie with Juliet.   290
Where be these enemies? Capulet, Montague,
See what a scourge is laid upon your hate,
That heaven finds means to kill your joys with love;
And I, for winking at your discords too,
Have lost a brace of kinsmen. All are punished.   295

Capulet   O brother Montague, give me thy hand.
This is my daughter's jointure, for no more
Can I demand.

Montague   But I can give thee more,
For I will raise her statue in pure gold,
That whiles Verona by that name is known,   300
There shall no figure at such rate be set
As that of true and faithful Juliet.

Capulet   As rich shall Romeo's by his lady's lie,
Poor sacrifices of our enmity.

Prince   A glooming peace this morning with it brings: 305
The sun for sorrow will not show his head.
Go hence to have more talk of these sad things.

**And I, for winking at your discords too,
Have lost a brace of kinsmen.**

Bristol Old Vic 1975

Some shall be pardoned, and some punished,
For never was a story of more woe
Than this of Juliet and her Romeo.   **310**

[*Exeunt*]

308 In Shakespeare's source for the story the Nurse is banished, the Apothecary is hanged and Friar Laurence is pardoned. What do you think of the justice of these sentences? Write or improve the scenes where the Prince interviews each of the three about their part in the story. Although the Prince would have dispensed justice himself without a court of law, you could set up a full trial to try each in turn.

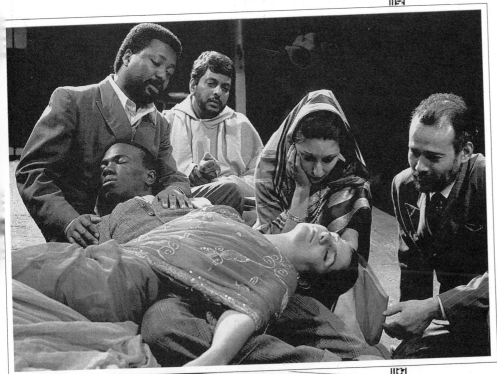

Albany Empire 1988

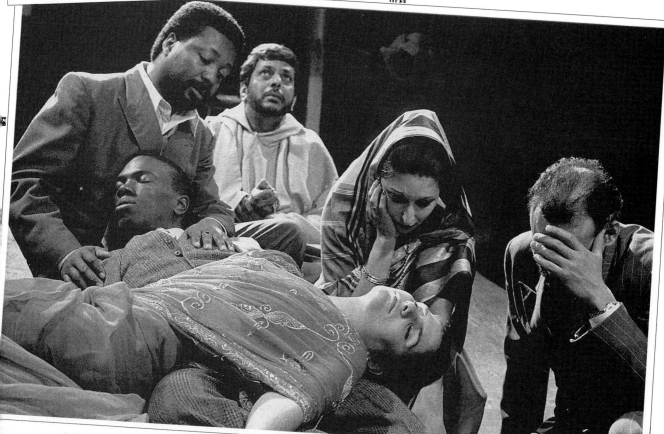

Sixty Activities and Questions

Below is a list of general activities which can be related to most areas of the play. Activities are also suggested in the marginal notes at specific points in the play where they are most appropriate to the action.

The activities have deliberately been made flexible so that they may be adapted to suit the requirements of the students. The list is not exhaustive, nor is it in any particular order, and ideas do overlap. The activities (or parts of activities) can be used as a basis for discussion, improvisation, written work, revision or whatever is considered important. Most are suitable for individual, paired or group work. The more traditional types of questions are included towards the end of the list, and may also be found among the marginal notes to the play.

1   Produce a speech, an episode, a scene, an act or the whole play.

2   Plan the lighting plot, the set design, the music or the sound for a speech, an episode, a scene, an act or the whole play.

3   Draw up a props list for a scene, an act or the whole play.

4   As director, write production notes for an actor who has to deliver one of the major speeches of the play. How will you advise him/her to say well-known words as if they are being thought of and spoken for the very first time?

5   As director, write production notes for actors in one episode or scene. Suggest how the actors may try to understand the thoughts and emotions in their own lives. For instance, during the first 17 lines of Act II Scene 5, Juliet is in a state of excited anxiety as she waits for the Nurse to return from her mission. We may not necessarily have been in Juliet's situation exactly, but we have all been at some time or other in a state of mind similar to Juliet's. Ask your actors about occasions when they have endured such unbearable anticipation. Get them to talk about it; or, if they tell you it is too personal to talk about, ask them to think about it and then, perhaps, write down their thoughts as personal writing (not to be shown to anyone).

6   Cast *Romeo and Juliet* from one of the following:
    a) Well-known actors and actresses. No restriction on choice: you are such a good director that they will all wish to be in your production if you cast them.
    b) Well-known public figures. It does not matter if they are not actors: you are casting them because you consider that their physical qualities, voice, manner (and, possibly, your perception of their characters – be careful!) fit the character in the play.
    c) Your class.
    d) Your friends and relations.
  Write a note justifying each piece of casting. For obvious reasons, you may wish to keep lists (c) and (d) private!

7   Write down which part in *Romeo and Juliet* you would most like to play, and say why.

8   In order to reduce its length, cut what you consider to be the less important lines from a scene or an act. Write notes justifying those cuts. What has been gained? What has been lost?

9   Rewrite the entire play in modern English in a version to last no longer than 15 minutes. Act it out in improvisation (that is, no scripts).

10   Discuss the significance of any one scene in the structure of the play as a whole.

11   If you have available the 1968 Franco Zeffirelli film version of *Romeo and Juliet*, play any one scene and compare it with Shakespeare's text. You will find that Zeffirelli has cut a great deal, sometimes because he has used visual images to take the place of some of the imagery in the original lines. Is he right to do this? What has been gained? What has been lost?

12   Discuss whether Shakespeare is best experienced on stage, on television/video or in the cinema. Is there any point in reading *Romeo and Juliet* if you can see it performed?

13   Discuss the evidence in *Romeo and Juliet* which suggests that, at the time the play was written, the authorities in London were worried about and keen to stamp out the growing fashion for duelling, a custom which had been imported from Italy.

14   Versions of the Romeo and Juliet story went back many centuries in Italy before it was made popular in England in 1562 through a translation in verse by Arthur Brooke. It was this which

Shakespeare used as source material for his play. Try to find a copy of Brooke's translation (extracts are printed at the back of the Arden edition of *Romeo and Juliet*, edited by Brian Gibbons and published by Methuen) and consider which aspects of the story Shakespeare has changed and why he has made such changes (for instance, the Nurse and Mercutio are insignificant figures in Brooke).

15   Following on from 14, we can see that Shakespeare used other writers as a source for his plays. Discuss in what ways he can still be seen as a great original writer.

16   Is *Romeo and Juliet* best produced in historical costume or in modern dress (as Michael Bogdanov's 1986 Royal Shakespeare Company productions)? What are the advantages and disadvantages of each approach?

17   *West Side Story* (1961) moves the Romeo and Juliet story to a poor area of New York. See the film (or, in the unlikely event of one being staged near you, a stage production) and then discuss how Shakespeare has been used as a source.

18   Write down in no more than one sentence an answer to the question 'What is *Romeo and Juliet* about?' Compare your answers as a way of exploring the dominant themes in the play.

    Remember that there is no correct answer, and that your answer, if different from other people's, may lead to just as valid an interpretation of the play. Always ask yourself what lines in the text support your view.

19   Take your idea of the main theme of the play, and write some notes on how it might affect your choice of set design, music, lighting, casting, pacing and other aspects of your production, were you to direct the play.

20   Choose one of the photographs or drawings in this book which you found helpful in understanding the play, and give your reasons for choosing it.

21   Choose a photograph which does not fit into your image of the play, and say why you consider it inappropriate.

22   Draw a picture of any moment in the play which is not illustrated in the book and which you feel is a good subject for illustration.

23   Photographs from various different productions are featured in this book. Say which production best fits your image of the play, and give your reasons. If possible, consider all the photographs from your chosen production.

24   See a stage production or a film version of *Romeo and Juliet*, and then say how far its interpretation agrees with your view of the play. You could concentrate on one character, theme, scene, episode, speech or idea. Or you could write a straightforward newspaper review of the production.

25   Build a set model for a production of *Romeo and Juliet*. It will be for a 'fixed' set: that is, the set remains constant for the whole play, and hence must be flexible and functional for the demands of every scene in the play.

26   Draw up a complete set of costume designs for the play. Be prepared to justify these in terms of your idea of what the play is about and your interpretation of the characters. You may choose to do a modern dress production.

27   Write or improvise a scene for the play which Shakespeare intended to insert into the action, but which he never got round to doing. You could try to write it in a pastiche of Shakespearean language, or you could stick to modern prose. The important thing is to make the events, characters, imagery and so forth consistent with the original play.

28 Design a poster, a programme cover or a whole programme for a production of *Romeo and Juliet*.

29 Write a letter from one character to another which might have been written at any point in the play.

30 Imagine that any one of the characters was in the habit of keeping a diary. Write up his/her entry after any one of the scenes in the play.

31 Write a newspaper report which might have been filed at any point in the play. It is important to decide where the journalist was at the time and how he came by his information. Do not include material which he could not possibly know. When you have finished, give your piece a brief, eye-catching headline.

32 Write a poem in response to any character, theme, episode, event, moment, or any other aspect of the play. The title of the poem must be a quotation from the play.

33 Make a chart showing in which of the 24 scenes each character appears. Then look closely at the chart and see if you can deduce any ideas about the way Shakespeare has constructed the plot of the play.

34 Characters often spend some time on the stage without speaking. However, as human beings, they will continue to think, particularly if the events enacted before them are in any way remarkable.
a) Write an 'inner' monologue for any one of the characters in which we see what he/she is thinking during one of the episodes in the play.
b) Write notes for the actor who is to play your chosen character, advising him how to register his thoughts during the episode (remember that acting is more than merely talking).

35 'Translate' any 14 lines from the play into good modern English. Try to retain both the meaning and the 'feel' of the original.

36 Write an obituary notice for any of the characters. You could write about one who dies during the course of *Romeo and Juliet*, in which case you must stick to the known facts of the play; or you could write about a character who survives the play, in which case you may imagine what happens to him/her in later life, but you must remain consistent to the character as established in *Romeo and Juliet*.

37 Think of as many *very brief* quotations as you can which are said by or about one of the characters. Then say how each quotation is significant.

38 Choose a character which you would like to play and prepare one of his/her speeches for audition. Use a tape-recorder and mirror to practise, and pay particular attention to tone of voice, pacing of the speech and facial gesture.

39 Make a quotation list comprising what you consider to be the ten most powerful images in *Romeo and Juliet*. Then, in the light of this list, discuss your impression of the overall tone of the play.

40 Invent a card- or board-game based on *Romeo and Juliet*. You could make it along the lines of the rules of an existing game, or it could be completely original. All hazard cards must bear an appropriate quotation from the play. One possible version is a 'Snakes and Ladders', in which the elements of Fate in the *Romeo and Juliet* play are used, ladders being available for good chance, snakes for bad.

(More details of this approach can be found in a journal called *Simulation/Games for Learning*, Volume 15, No 3, edited by Alan Coote, Polytechnic of Wales, Pontypridd, Mid-Glamorgan CF37 1DL.)

41 Invite an actor or director who has been involved with a production of *Romeo and Juliet* to come and talk about the experience.

42 Write a review of the first night of *Romeo and Juliet* in the Globe Theatre. You could include comments on how the Elizabethan audience received the play.

43 Write out the transcript of an interview with William Shakespeare, who is pleased with the favourable reception at the first night of his new play. You could brief one of your friends to play the part of Shakespeare in the interview and, like many journalists, use a tape-recorder to record the conversation.

44 Take any line in the play and practise saying it in different ways, varying the words upon which you place stress. Consider which version you think most satisfactory, and say why.

45 What Shakespeare wrote in his plays were the thoughts and opinions of his characters, not of himself. However, we can see from a play such as *Romeo and Juliet* the breadth of his knowledge and understanding.

Take a speech, episode, scene, act or the whole play and, with close reference to the text, show what we can deduce about Shakespeare's knowledge and understanding.

46 Say in what ways Shakespeare encouraged his audience to use its imagination. Look closely at the language of *Romeo and Juliet*.

47 Examine closely any one soliloquy in the play, and then discuss the dramatic functions of soliloquies. How are they useful in putting over what dialogue cannot do?

48 Discuss what you mean by 'tragedy'. In what sense is *Romeo and Juliet* a tragedy? Is the tragedy a result of Fate, against which the characters can do little? Or do they bring the tragedy upon themselves? Or is it a mixture of both – and, if so, in what proportions?

Is life more tragic when people bring about their own downfall?

49 Discuss the comic elements in *Romeo and Juliet*. Why do you think they are there?

50 Which two characters in the play do you find most interesting? Why? Do you find them and their actions understandable? Do you feel that you want to judge them, or can you view them with compassion? Do you sympathise with them? Can you go as far as identifying (empathising) with them – that is, can you, so to speak, climb inside them and know what it is like to go around with their thoughts, hopes, anxieties, fears, etc., in your head?

51 Choose any illustration in this edition which has no caption. Then search the text of the play to find a suitable caption.

52 'The Nurse, Capulet and Friar Laurence all love Juliet, yet all contribute towards her death.' Show how far this is true by referring closely to words and incidents in the play.

53 Write out a speech from the play and then scan it, putting accent marks over the syllables which you think should be stressed.

54 'At the beginning of the play Romeo is a love-sick boy; by the end he is a man.' Do you agree?

55 *Romeo and Juliet* can be very exciting and moving in performance. Which two incidents in the play would you select as particularly (a) dramatic and (b) moving? Support your choice with detailed reference to the text.

56 '*Romeo and Juliet* is distinguished by the vitality and variety of its language and of its characters.' Discuss, basing your answer on an analysis of either language or character.

57 Show how Shakespeare's poetry helps to create the right atmosphere for the events of the play.

58 Recite (not necessarily from memory) your favourite lines from *Romeo and Juliet*. Say why you like them.

59 Early in the play Romeo says: *Here's much to do with hate, but more with love.* Consider the play in the light of this remark, examining the nature of hatred and love in the play and the effect they have upon people.

60 Look at the pictures on page 102 and decide which part of the play they each illustrate. Provide suitable captions.

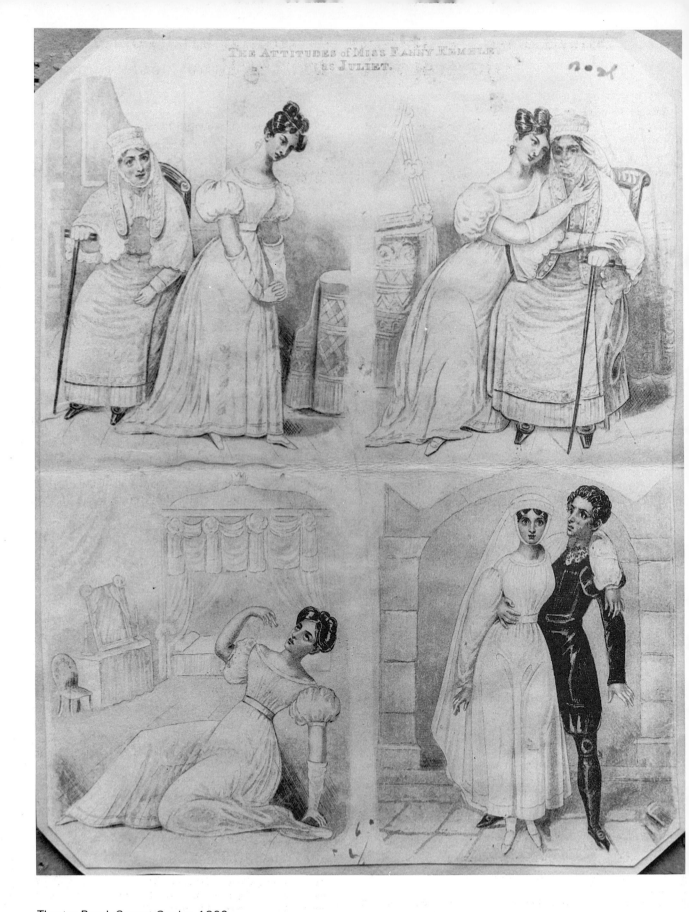

THE ATTITUDES of MISS FANNY KEMBLE as JULIET.

Theatre Royal, Covent Garden 1829

Notes on Productions of *Romeo and Juliet* Illustrated in this Edition

Albany Empire 1988
Director: Teddy Kiendl • Romeo: Carlton Chance • Juliet: Janet Steel

For further information contact: Publicity Manager, The Albany Empire, Douglas Way, London SE8 4AG. Tel: 01–691 8016

Bristol Old Vic 1949 (at the Theatre Royal)
Director: Allan Davies • Romeo: John Byron • Juliet: Jane Wenham
Bristol Old Vic 1959 (at the Theatre Royal)
Director: John Hale • Romeo: Paul Massie • Juliet: Annette Crosbie
Bristol Old Vic 1966 (at the Theatre Royal)
Director: Val May • Romeo: Gawn Grainger • Juliet: Jane Asher
Bristol Old Vic 1975 (at the Little Theatre)
Director: David Horlock • Romeo: John Nolan • Juliet: Paula Wilcox
Bristol Old Vic 1983 (at the New Vic)
Director: Anthony Cornish • Romeo: Peter Woodward • Juliet: Miranda Foster

For further information contact: Publicity Officer, Bristol Old Vic, Theatre Royal, Bristol BS1 4ED. Tel: 0272 277466

Citizens Theatre 1975
Director: David Hayman • Romeo: Oengus Macnamara • Juliet: Johanna Kirby

For further information contact: Press and Publicity Manager, Citizens Theatre, Gorbals, Glasgow G5 9DS. Tel: 041–429 5561/0022

Compass Theatre Company 1987–8
Director: Neil Sissons • Romeo: David Westbrook • Juliet: Helen Schlesinger

For further information contact: Administrator, Compass Theatre Company, The Leadmill, 6/7 Leadmill Road, Sheffield S1 4SF. Tel: 0742 755328

Crucible Theatre 1984
Director: Euan Smith • Romeo: John Skitt • Juliet: Christine Cox

For further information contact: Publicity Officer, Crucible Theatre, 55 Norfolk Street, Sheffield S1 1DA. Tel: 0742 760621

Gateway Theatre 1976
Director: Christopher Honer • Romeo: David Sibley • Juliet: Deborah Hurst

For further information contact: Publicity Officer, Gateway Theatre, Hamilton Place, Chester CH1 2BH. Tel: 0244 44238

Lyceum Theatre 1882
Romeo: Henry Irving • Juliet: Ellen Terry
Lyceum Theatre 1908
Romeo: Matheson Long • Juliet: Nora Kerin
Lyric Theatre 1919
Romeo: Basil Sydney • Juliet: Doris Keane
New Theatre 1935
Romeo: Laurence Olivier/John Gielgud • Juliet: Peggy Ashcroft

For further information contact: The Shakespeare Birthplace Trust, The Shakespeare Centre, Stratford-upon-Avon, Warwickshire CV37 6QW. Tel: 0789 204016

Orchard Theatre 1986
Director: Nigel Bryant • Romeo: Duncan Law • Juliet: Robin McCaffrey

For further information contact: Marketing Officer, Orchard Theatre, 108 Newport Road, Barnstaple, Devon EX32 9BA. Tel: 0271 71475/73356

Redgrave Theatre 1974
Director: Ian Mullins • Romeo: Martin Connor • Juliet: Sammie Winmill

For further information contact: Publicity and Marketing Assistant, Redgrave Theatre, Brightwells, Farnham, Surrey GU9 7SB. Tel: 0252 727000

Royal Shakespeare Company 1961
Director: Peter Hall • Romeo: Brian Murray • Juliet: Dorothy Tutin

Royal Shakespeare Company 1967
Director: Karolos Koun • Romeo: Ian Holm • Juliet: Estelle Kohler
Royal Shakespeare Company 1976
Director: Trevor Nunn with Barry Kyle • Romeo: Ian McKellan • Juliet: Francesca Annis
Royal Shakespeare Company 1983–4
Director: John Caird • Romeo: Daniel Day-Lewis • Juliet: Amanda Root
Royal Shakespeare Company 1984 (at The Other Place)
Director: John Caird • Romeo: Simon Templeman • Juliet: Amanda Root
Royal Shakespeare Company 1986
Director: Michael Bogdanov • Romeo: Sean Bean • Juliet: Niamh Cusack
Royal Shakespeare Company 1989 (at the Swan Theatre)
Director: Terry Hands • Romeo: Mark Rylance • Juliet: Georgia Slowe

For further information contact: Publicity Officer, Royal Shakespeare Theatre, Stratford-upon-Avon, Warwickshire CV37 6BB. Tel: 0789 296655. Or The Shakespeare Birthplace Trust, The Shakespeare Centre, Stratford-upon-Avon, Warwickshire CV37 6QW. Tel: 0789 204016

Royal Theatre Northampton 1982
Director: Michael Napier Brown • Romeo: Jonathan Dockar-Drysdale • Juliet: Yolanda Vasquez

For further information contact: Publicity Officer, Royal Theatre, 15 Guildhall Road, Northampton NN1 1EA. Tel: 0604 38343

Temba Theatre Company 1988
Director: Alby James • Romeo: David Harewood • Juliet: Georgia Slowe

For further information contact: Publicity Officer, Temba Theatre Company, Dominion House, 101 Southwark Street, London SE1 0JH. Tel: 01–261 0991

Theatre Royal, Covent Garden 1753
Romeo: Spranger Barry • Juliet: Mrs Cibber
Theatre Royal, Covent Garden 1784
Romeo: Richard Wroughton • Juliet: Mrs Kemble
Theatre Royal, Covent Garden 1822
Romeo: Charles Kemble • Juliet: Miss F H Kelly

Theatre Royal, Covent Garden 1829
Romeo: Charles Kemble • Juliet: Miss Jarman

For further information contact: The Shakespeare Birthplace Trust, The Shakespeare Centre, Stratford-upon-Avon, CV37 6QW. Tel: 0789 204016

Victoria Theatre 1968
Director: Peter Cheeseman • Romeo: Chris Martin • Juliet: Susan Glanville

For further information contact: Press and Public Relations Officer, New Victoria Theatre, Etruria Road, Newcastle-under-Lyme, Staffordshire ST5 0JG. Tel: 0782 717539

York Theatre Royal 1988
Director: Jonathan Petherbridge • Romeo: Sean Gilder • Juliet: Maria Gough

For further information contact: Marketing Director, York Theatre Royal, St Leonard's Place, York Y01 2HD. Tel: 0904 658162

Young Vic 1987–8
Directors: David Thacker and Jeremy Bell • Romeo: Clive Owen • Juliet: Sarah-Jane Fenton

For further information contact: Publicity Officer, The Young Vic, 66 The Cut, London SE1 8LZ. Tel: 01-633 0133

Zeffirelli 1968 (Paramount Pictures Corporation)
Director: Franco Zeffirelli • Romeo: Leonard Whiting • Juliet: Olivia Hussey

For further information contact: British Film Institute, Stills Library, 21 Stephen Street, London W1P 1PL. Tel: 01-255 1444